What people are saying about this manual

"I have read your manual on starting your own concierge business. Let me tell you - it was wonderful. The examples and all of the tried and true advice made sense. I have read too many home business books that are too general, even if the table of contents suggests otherwise. As a result, I am working on my business plan and have developed a name "Spirit Concierge" which I intend to register within the next week. So thank you for putting together exactly what I needed. Thanks again for a wonderfully written "How to..." guide. It made it easy to get started." **Carla Mandell, Spirit Concierge**

"Katharine, I received the manual the day after I ordered it , which was great because I was anxious to get it. Once I picked it up, I could not put it down until I finished. I was extremely pleased and excited about the contents of the manual. You thought of everything! Now thanks to you, I have a more focused vision of what I want to do and how to go about getting there. It is the ONLY manual I have recommended for those thinking about starting a concierge service. Thank you for providing such an excellent and thorough source of information for those of us struggling to find material for this business." **Ineavelle Middleton, Middco Go-For Services**

"Your book is detailed and easy to understand and serves as a model for other young business entrepreneurs. Outstanding and fantastic job!!!!! Thank you." **Dennia Awen, California**

"I read your book from cover to cover and thoroughly enjoyed it. You have done a magnificent job highlighting all the ins and outs of this business." **Grace Howes, North Carolina**

"Really want to thank God for choosing you and Ron to be the forerunner in the concierge business. The information that you have in your book was so helpful. I was able to focus and get a better insight on the business by following the guidelines that you set in place." **Christopher Scott, Point of Contact, Nashville, TN**

"I read your book and found it very insightful, educational, and instructional. It played a tremendous role in laying down some of the ground work and planning for our "soon to be launched" endeavor. Thanks again!" **Bernard L. Lewis, Synergee LLC, New York**

"I have recently ordered your *Concierge Manual* and am learning so much, which is extremely informative and more useful than I could have hoped. Thank you sharing your expertise with the rest of us. You are certainly a role model and mentor to this new growing field. Thank you!" **Jennifer Stoops, Florida**

"I received my manual—and I am well pleased! It is full of vital information, some things I never considered or thought of. Thank you again for writing such a well informed manual." **Joyce Thomas, California**

"Purchasing your manual and contracts has been by far the best investment we have made into our business! Thank you so much for the invaluable information and all the support you have given us! It is nice to know there still is service after the sale." **Steven Meyer, Ohio**

"A great investment in my business. I found the book to be straight forward and to the point. It is full of valuable information. Especially for newbies with lots of questions. No fluff in this one. Thank you!" **Vikki White, The Organized Life**

"Thank you for your great book! Event hough some parts of it have to be a little different on the way of thinking here in Denmark, it has saved me from a lot of guesswork." **Jimmy Therkelsen, Personal Concierge, Denmark**

"I received my manual from you a couple of months ago and it has been fantastic. My partner and I have a meeting with a property manager on Tuesday. We could not have done it without your book! **Tia DeVoll, Hill Country Concierge**

"Thanks so much for the <u>detailed</u> book. Now, I am *less* scared and *more* excited! I enjoyed our conversation, your encouragement and personable approach is refreshing. Got to go...lots of work ahead of me!" **Rhonda Kositzky, ASAP Personal Concierge**

"I received your book the day after I ordered it, which was amazing in itself, but the content! You have saved me from so many trial and error mis-steps and given me so many good ideas! Thanks so much for sharing your knowledge and experiences with people like me who want to learn. I've read the *Manual* twice, stopping only to read *God, is that you?"* **Patty Dickerson, Energy Direct Communications, Dallas, Texas**

I just wanted to thank you for this wonderful book! I now have direction for my business, and you made me feel I really could do it! Thank you once again!" **Jeniffer Karas, ETC Enterprises**

"I have just finished reading *The Concierge Manual,* I enjoyed it, thank you! I really enjoy your writing style - clear and concise! It was well worth the cost! Your book helped give us the inspiration to take this challenge, and for that we are very grateful!" **Jim Towers**

"I'd just like to say thank you for the great detail in your book *The Concierge Manual* - I received it a couple of months ago and read it within two days. Now with the fantastic help gained from your book, I am now at the stage where I hope to be starting my own concierge within the next month. Thank you again!" **Liz Dunn,** *It's Dunn 4 U*, **Melbourne Australia**

Other Books by Katharine C. Giovanni

God, is that you?

The In-House Concierge Manual

101 Great Ways to Improve Your Life: Volume 3
  (Contributing Author)

Newsletters

The Triangle Times

The Concierge Manual

A Step-by-Step Guide on How to Start Your Own
Concierge Service and/or Lifestyle Management
Company

Third Edition

Katharine C. Giovanni

with Ron Giovanni

NewRoad Publishing   Wake Forest, NC

Published By: NewRoad Publishing
3650 Rogers Road, #328, Wake Forest, NC 27587
Tel: 919-453-2850
Email: Ron@NewRoadPublishing.com

First Edition 2000
Second Edition 2002
Third Edition: November 2006

An application to register this book for cataloging has been submitted to the Library of Congress.

Third Edition
ISBN   1-931109-07-9
          978-931109-07-9

Printed in the United States of America
Cover Design by Candice Goble

To Eleanor and Joan

Their incredible strength, courage and dignity
taught me to never give up,
no matter what.

About the Author ...

Katharine C. Giovanni

Author, Consultant, Speaker and International Concierge Training Expert

Katharine has been a meeting/event planner and concierge for over 20 years and has set up several successful businesses including Triangle Concierge, Triangle International, and NewRoad Publishing. She is Triangle Concierge's senior trainer and speaker and is co-author of their best-selling book *The Concierge Manual* as well as the author of the *In-House Concierge Manual.* Katharine is also one of the developers of TriTrax, the world's premier concierge software.

Katharine is the Chairman of the Board of the International Concierge and Errand Association (ICEA).

A dynamic public speaker, Katharine has been a speaker at seminars and conferences around the country, and has appeared on both radio and television including ABC News Nightline and The Joey Reynolds show. She is also the author of the acclaimed inspirational book *God, is that you?*

Raised in New York City, Katharine has a B.A. from Lake Forest College and currently lives in North Carolina with her husband Ron and two children.

Katharine can be reached through her websites at www.TriangleConcierge.com; www.katharinegiovanni.com or www.TriangleInternational.com.

With assistance from ...

Ron Giovanni

Consultant, Publisher, Speaker and International Concierge Training Expert

Ron has been in the customer service, sales and operations field for over 25 years and and has set up several successful businesses including Triangle Concierge, Triangle International, and NewRoad Publishing.

Ron has been teaching people how to start their own business since 1998. He is responsible for Triangle's operations including meeting planning, travel management, internet and web solutions, sales and marketing, research and development. He is also the co-developer of TriTrax, the world's premier concierge software.

Ron is President and Founder of NewRoad Publishing and has published four books at last count. He has also produced software and workshop audio CD's.

Ron can be reached through his websites at www.TriangleConcierge.com or www.NewRoadPublishing.com

I owe my success to having listened respectfully
to the very best advice,
and then going away and doing the exact opposite.

G. K. Chesterton

DISCLAIMERS & LEGAL NOTICES

Information Accuracy

The author and NewRoad Publishing make every effort to ensure that all information presented in this book is correct. However, we do not guarantee the accuracy of the information contained in this book, and reliance on information provided in this book is solely at your own risk. Every effort has been made to make this book as complete as possible; however, it may yet contain mistakes, both typographical and substantive. Therefore, this book should be used only as a general guide and not as the ultimate source of information on the concierge industry.

Disclaimer of Warranties

THIS BOOK IS PROVIDED SOLELY ON AN "AS-IS" BASIS AND THE USE OF THE INFORMATION CONTAINED HEREIN IS AT YOUR SOLE RISK. EXCEPT TO THE EXTENT REQUIRED BY ANY MANDATORY APPLICABLE LAW, THIS BOOK AND THE INFORMATION CONTAINED HEREIN ARE NOT SUBJECT TO ANY WARRANTY OR CONDITION, EXPRESS OR IMPLIED, INCLUDING, WITHOUT LIMITATION, ANY WARRANTY OF MERCHANTABILITY, SATISFACTORY QUALITY, FITNESS FOR A PARTICULAR PURPOSE OR USE, OR NON-INFRINGEMENT.

NEITHER THE AUTHOR NOR NEWROAD PUBLISHING GUARANTEES THE ACCURACY OR COMPLETENESS OF ANY INFORMATION CONTAINED IN THIS BOOK. NEITHER THE AUTHOR NOR NEWROAD PUBLISHING ASSUMES ANY LIABILITY OR RESPONSIBILITY FOR ANY ERRORS OR OMISSIONS IN THE INFORMATION CONTAINED IN THE BOOK.

NEITHER THE AUTHOR NOR NEWROAD PUBLISHING MAKES ANY REPRESENTATIONS OR WARRANTIES OF ANY KIND, EXPRESS OR IMPLIED, AS TO THE BOOK OR THE INFORMATION CONTAINED HEREIN OR THE RESULTS THAT MAY BE OBTAINED FROM THE USE OF INFORMATION CONTAINED IN THE BOOK. THE BOOK AND THE INFORMATION CONTAINED THEREIN ARE NOT, AND SHOULD NOT BE CONSIDERED TO BE, PRESENTING YOU WITH ANY TYPE OF BUSINESS OPPORTUNITY OFFERING OR ITS EQUIVALENT. THE BOOK AND THE INFORMATION CONTAINED THEREIN ARE NOT INTENDED TO REPRESENT OR WARRANT TO YOU THAT YOU CAN OPERATE A

Acknowledgements

Many special thanks go to my husband and business partner, Ron Giovanni, for all the help, love, wisdom and support he gave me in putting together this book.

Many thanks also go to:

Candice Goble for her support, wisdom and extraordinary talent. The cover she designed for this book is absolutely incredible.

Connie Domino for her support, wisdom and awesome talent.

Doug and Polly Johns for teaching me about customer service and for providing such a wonderful example for all of us to follow.

Last, but not least, to my boys for they are the wind beneath my sails.

Thank you! This book could not have been written without you. You have my most sincere thanks.

Katharine

A journey of a thousand miles begins with a single step.

Lao-tzu

Table of Contents

Success can make you go one of two ways.
It can make you a prima donna,
or it can smooth the edges,
take away the insecurities,
let the nice things come out.

Barbara Walters

Forward

Before I begin explaining how to start your own concierge business, I think it might be helpful if I explained how Ron and I got started in this business.

I have been a meeting and event planner for over 20 years and have set up five successful businesses: Meeting Planning Plus, Triangle Concierge, Triangle International, NewRoad Publishing and XPACS. After graduating with a B.A. from Lake Forest College in 1984, I began my career by working for the American Society of Corporate Secretaries from 1986 until 1994. ASCS is a society whose members include Corporate Secretaries, CEO's and Treasurers of the major Fortune 500 companies around the country.

While at ASCS, I was responsible for organizing and implementing corporate conferences, seminars, board/committee meetings, exhibits, and banquets across the United States and in Canada. The conferences I organized included banquets, tours, spouse programs, educational programs, as well as children's programs. I chose the site, developed program logistics, arranged ground transportation, selected speakers and provided clients with written materials that included brochures and conference materials.

I was also the official "gopher" for all those VIP's doing whatever they needed done. Whether it was meeting them at the airport, doing an errand, getting them some lunch or having their handouts copied and collated. In fact, more often than not, I was the one adding a last minute item to all those attendee workbooks. Isn't this beginning to sound like concierge work?

Remember that in those days there was no such thing as a corporate concicrgc, so whcn somconc nccded work of this sort done they called a meeting planner. Meeting planners are very used to wearing 30 hats while doing a balancing act on the high wire. No request is too outrageous for the planner because she/he becomes very adept at finding the hard-to-find and doing the impossible. Catering to the needs of VIP's, speakers, meeting attendees, co-workers and even family is what a meeting planner does. Today, that same individual can also be called a "concierge."

Working for ASCS proved invaluable for establishing my own business. My experience gave me the foundation I needed in dealing with the officers of the corporate world. Never underestimate how important that understanding is. It can make or break a contract.

My husband and I started Meeting Planning Plus in 1995. Over the years, we began to realize that we were doing much more concierge-type work than meeting planning. We also learned that the concierge services industry had the potential for taking off and was fast becoming the wave of the future. So after a few modifications, we changed our company name and targeted concierge services. Triangle Concierge was born in the fall of 1998.

As I began Triangle Concierge, it soon became apparent that there were no resource materials available on the market to help me get started. There were no books on the subject or consultants to approach. Frankly, I was unable to locate any helpful information. I was on my own. It took me approximately a year to teach myself and research how to start a concierge service (truly the ultimate of self-taught) and we were ready to open for business.

Almost immediately the telephone started to ring. First one call, then ten. People started calling and emailing me from all over the world asking me to spare just a moment of my time to tell them how I started my business, and I told them. I spent hours answering each question as best as I could.

Until one day my husband overheard me and asked me what I was doing. When I told him he said, "Why are you doing it for free?"

Good question! Why indeed was I?

So, based on my expertise in meeting planning, concierge work, and the fact that I had started two successful companies, I decided to write a manual on how to start your own concierge business. Just because I learned everything the hard way doesn't mean that others have to. There was most certainly a huge need for the information because in those early days there was no information at all. Anywhere.

I spent the next few months writing the first edition of the *Concierge Manual*. Once the book began to sell, the phone calls increased dramatically in a matter of weeks. I received calls and e-mails from all over the world from people wanting more services and information, asking questions and the like. As a result of all this, we realized that we had to make a decision regarding our company's focus.

At the time, I was spending 90% of my time consulting, and 10% trying to grow my local concierge business. So, after a long discussion, in 1999, Triangle Concierge, the concierge consultants, was born. We officially turned ourselves into full-time concierge consultants and let go of our local concierge business.

The materials that I developed for the original Triangle Concierge is now being shared with the world through this book. The information, forms, brochures, sales letters, proposals and all the information that I learned over the past 20 years has gone into these pages so that others do not have to make the same mistakes that I did.

Today, I've consulted thousands of companies and individuals from over 40 countries and every U.S. State. Triangle Concierge was one of the first two companies in the world to do concierge consulting. In fact, several more have actually popped up since the publication of our first edition in 1998. Medical and legal professionals have been specializing for years – we just did the same thing.

It is my ultimate hope that the ideas that are presented here will help you set up your own business. Since there are about 10,001 ways to set up a concierge business, some of the opinions presented in this book will help you, and some will not. Review the entire manual, use those ideas that work for you and discard the ones that don't. Owning your own business is hard work, but it can be very rewarding and is never dull.

So my advice is to take it one day at a time and to not lose your focus. Stay focused on what you are doing and where you would like to go. If you find yourself getting discouraged because the clients are not coming as fast as you would like, take heart because persistence is the key to this business. Assume that your business is going to soar! Do not say you are going to just give it a try ... simply do it and make it happen. If you assume that your business is going to be a HUGE success, and you think this thought with every bone in your body, then it will. You will run into obstacles along the way of course, but assume that these will work themselves out, and somehow they will.

I have been an entrepreneur for many years now, and I can tell you from personal experience that it has not always an easy road, but it has definitely been worth it and I would do it again in a heartbeat. Being your own boss, never dealing with rush hour traffic, office politics, misunderstandings with your boss, and never having to wonder if the sludge on the bottom of the coffeepot is drinkable is wonderful! Tell me, where else can you go to work in your bathrobe?

Simply make the choice to be a success and you will. Feel the decision and move forward. KNOW that you can do it and you will!!! Have no doubts!

Why?

Because if you have faith you can do anything.

Katharine C. Giovanni

A Concierge/Lifestyle Manager is a Purveyor of Time.

Ron Giovanni

Introduction

What exactly is a concierge? Depends on who you ask. Entrepreneur Magazine's *Concierge Start-up Guide* gives the following definition. It's really the best one I've ever read, and I've read a lot of them!

"Although more and more people are becoming familiar with the term "concierge," very few know where this customer-service based profession originated. The word "concierge" evolves from the French comte des cierges, *the "keeper of the candler," a term that referred to the servant who attended to the whims of visiting noblemen at medieval castles. Eventually, the name "concierge" came to stand for keeper of the keys at public buildings, especially hotels. There is even a famous prison in Paris that is called The Conciergerie, in honor of the warden who kept the keys and assigned cells to the inmates."*

Merriam-Webster Online Dictionary offers this definition …

French, from Old French, prob from (assumed) Vulgar Latin conservius, alteration of Latin conservus fellow slave, from com- + servus slave. 1 : a resident in an apartment building especially in France who serves as doorkeeper, landlord's representative, and janitor. 2 : a usually multilingual hotel staff member who handles luggage and mail, makes reservations, and arranges tours.

Lastly, a client of mine from Mexico tells me that in his country, the word "concierge" means janitor!!!

Regardless of the origin, hotels from around the world were the first ones to adopt the concierge idea and offer the service to their guests. Today, independent concierge companies have brought this ancient service to the modern world so that now everyone has access to them.

So what exactly is a concierge?? I think the short version here is that it is simply another word for personal assistant.

The concierge business is growing by leaps and bounds, and concierge companies are literally popping up all over corporate America. Concierge services have been available for some time, but were historically only found in hotel lobbies. Recently, however, these services have begun to emerge in the corporate world.

The concierge industry itself is only about 15-20 years old and started with a few brave pioneers who took the hotel concierge idea and decided to offer it to the corporate world. I have been in the field since 1998 and when I started there were perhaps 50 or so concierge services around the U.S. Today, I suspect there are thousands. I have nothing to base these numbers on except my personal experience in the field. You can actually see the phenomenal growth by looking at my company's numbers. Triangle Concierge began in 1998 with a dozen clients. Today, we have thousands of clients from over 40 countries and every US state.

You can now find concierge services everywhere ... in hospitals, malls, corporations, apartment buildings, office buildings, airports, colleges, associations, churches, and on and on and on. You could sum up the state of the industry in two words - extraordinary growth.

We all do a balancing act every day, and since most of us don't have a personal assistant to make the phone calls and run the errands for us, we try and cram them into the weekend and on our lunch hour during the week. In fact, many people feel that there are simply not enough hours in the day to get everything done. Right?

Well, help has arrived!!!

Although the concierge industry is fairly new, the number of companies that are catering to time-starved people is skyrocketing as is the customer demand for such businesses. Why? Simple. People are trying to squeeze 36 hours into a 24-hour day.

Companies around the world are also getting into the act. They are not only starting to use corporate concierges, but are making them a part of their corporate benefit packages. They are reasoning correctly that the less time people spend running personal errands during the workday, the more time they can spend at their desks and subsequently with their families at night.

We all have to do that balancing act every day, and although everyone's schedule is different, it may go something like this ... Once you get breakfast on the table and pack the children off to school, you rush off to work only to get slammed by rush hour traffic. At lunch you make some personal telephone calls, run to the drug store, dry cleaners, buy your son a new knapsack for school and quickly return the video you rented last week. Then you grab a fast-food sandwich on the way back to work. Sound familiar yet?

After work you pick up the kids, take them to their various after-school activities, make dinner, and afterwards make appointments at the doctor, dentist and the vet. Then you make some more telephone calls, a golf tee time for next weekend because your father-in-law is coming, and take the groceries and prescription you purchased after work over to your elderly mother's house. You then put her groceries away, tidy up her house, feed the cat, walk the dog and make her a quick meal.

Tired yet? Wouldn't it be great to have a personal assistant who could do this stuff for you? An affordable one?

Most people, unfortunately, do not have their own assistants so they try to cram these little errands into their after-work hours and already busy Saturdays. More often than not, however, they creep into regular work time. After all, most people who you need to do business with do business during regular work hours, right?

In fact, sometimes it just seems like there are not enough hours in the day. We are simply exhausted from the increasing demands placed on us at work and by the daily commute, so at the end of the day we drag ourselves home to give only sleepy-eyed attention to our families.

According to a study of the U.S. work force released by the Families and Work Institute (statistics found online at www.entrepreneurmag. com):

- The average worker spends 44 hours per week on the job.
- 36 % of workers say they often feel completely used up at the end of the workday.
- 85% of workers have daily family responsibilities to go home to.
- 78% of married workers have spouses who are also employed.
- Weekends are consumed by errands and housekeeping.
- 70% of all parents feel that they don't spend enough time with their children.

Down time? What's that? No one has the time for it anymore.

When looking at these statistics, it is easy to see why time has become the commodity of the century and will be even more so in the decades to come. The popularity of concierge services stems from the fact that people are stressed out, overworked, and need help dealing with life so they can spend their free time nurturing themselves and their families. As good workers become harder to find, businesses are looking for concierge services to offer as perks to keep valuable employees happy.

Working Mother Magazine published a list of the top 100 companies to work for, and they all seem to have one thing in common, they all offer work/life benefits to their employees. Companies are finally focusing on the fact that people cannot do it all and they need help. Consequently, companies are adding work life benefits such as day care centers, job sharing, dry cleaning pick-up/delivery, leave for new parents and many are letting you work from home. Some companies are even adding on-site company chefs who will cook dinner for you to take home at the end of the day! Others are developing programs to help you care for your elderly parents, and of course, concierge services are being added as part of corporate benefits packages.

The work/life idea is taking off like the proverbial brush fire and is reaching almost every corner of the United States. When we started in 1998 there were only a handful of concierge companies around the nation. Today, with work/life programs becoming more and more popular, there are probably thousands with more popping up every day. In-house concierge departments are also popping up, as are on-site (or lobby) concierges.

People are embracing concierge and errand services because they give individuals more time to spend both at their desks and with their families at night. It is the classic win-win situation In addition, real estate management companies are offering on-site/lobby concierge services to their tenants to add value to their properties and increase their marketability.

These "lobby" concierge concierge companies are placing concierge services in office buildings to provide personal and business services to tenants. The concierges offer a host of services that include picking up dry cleaning, managing catered business lunches, picking up theater tickets, ordering dinner and shopping for clothes. They become the friendly faces that clients see on a daily basis that can help them manage their lives. Personal service is the hallmark of the concierge business.

One question the media always seem to ask me when they call is where I think the concierge industry will be in a few years. Well, I can best answer that question through a little history.

After I graduated from college in 1984, I found a job working as an administrative assistant to a meeting planner. After a few months I quickly found out that not only did I enjoy the work, but I had an aptitude for it. In those days, however, there were no books or courses you could take to learn meeting planning. You just learned it from the bottom up while in the field. Not many people knew what a meeting planner was back then, and certainly no one was teaching the subject in college.

Today, meetings are a billion dollar industry. Colleges are offering majors in meeting planning, seminars are being taught around the world, associations have been created for meeting planners, and hundreds of books have been written on the subject. The concierge industry is going to go the same way as the meeting industry, it just isn't going to take 15 years to do it. In fact, I predict it will only take about 5 years or less.

Soon, most companies around the nation will be offering concierge services as part of a benefits package. Apartment buildings and businesses will offer concierge services to tenants and businesses, and everyone will not only have access to a service near them, but they will be able to afford it. Most of all, they will also be able to finally spell and pronounce the word "concierge."

Here are just a few of the services that are currently offered by concierge services around the country:

- Personal Shopping including dry cleaning pick-up/delivery and grocery shopping
- Search for tickets to concerts and special events
- Transportation Services
- Business Referral Service
- Restaurant Recommendations and Reservations
- Pet services
- Senior care
- Modified house sitting
- Travel and Vacation Planning
- Meeting and Event Planning

The sky is the limit! There are dozens and dozens of things you can do here.

Certainly the concierge industry is the wave of the future.

Never continue in a job you don't enjoy.
If you're happy in what you're doing,
you'll like yourself, you'll have inner peace.
And if you have that, along with physical health,
you will have had more success
than you could possibly have imagined.

Johnny Carson

Chapter 1

What skills do I need to become a successful concierge?

You have to be the type of person who will labor until the work is done no matter what time it is. If you are the type of person who leaves work at exactly 5:00 p.m. no matter what, then may I suggest that you read this section very carefully before embarking on this new venture. The client always comes first, and if that same client needs some work finished by a certain day, then you need to be sure to finish it, on time.

Experience in sales, marketing, meeting/event planning, human resources and customer service are all great things to have, but are not essential. I know of an excellent concierge who was an engineer in his "past life," and his business is flourishing. In the beginning you will be everyone — the bookkeeper, secretary, receptionist, errand runner, meeting planner, webmaster, business owner, mail room clerk, administrative assistant, president and chief bottle washer. You are the classic Girl (or Boy) Friday who does everything for everyone.

There is no such thing as a time clock when you own your own business, just like there is no such thing as a paycheck. I jokingly complained for months that I was the classic case of "overworked and never paid," but if you can hold on, the payoff is big because eventually your concierge business will soar. In this business you can't wait for things to come to you, you have to go to them. You need to be able to talk to virtually anyone about anything. The type of person who can have a conversation with a post in the subway.

You should be able to radiate enthusiasm when talking about your business, and you need to be able to work steadily day and night without complaint.

When you own your own business you have to be everything to everyone. If you have children at home then you not only have to balance everything in your new business, but you also have to find time for the kids. I myself have a husband and two children and finding balance makes me feel like a tightrope walker sometimes, but it is worth it.

The good news is that owning my own business allows me to set my own schedule and I can be there for my kids when they need me. It gives me the freedom to come and go as I please and work at my own schedule. Further, since my office is in my home the commute is great! No more rushing home at 3:00 p.m. (breaking every speed record in the book, by the way) so I can make it to the school bus on time. I also always carry my cell phone with me so I can return telephone calls and speak with clients anytime day or night. This may appear to be intrusive, and at times it feels that way, but in my opinion it is essential in business that the client feels that their needs come first.

The downside to this? When there is a blizzard outside and everyone else gets the day off because the roads are completely impassable, you are the only lucky one on the block who can actually get to work. Actually, this might be a good thing!

So, what type of person do you have to be? Outgoing, friendly, completely honest, open, talkative, and enthusiastic. A real "go-getter" if you will. You need to be willing to work crazy hours doing seemingly crazy things, and you absolutely must follow through.

You need to be able to wear 50 hats at once. You need to be able to not only find the impossible, but do the impossible. You need to be able to talk on the phone, work on the computer, answer a question from one of your staffers and chew gum all at the same time. And, most critically, you need to be willing to sacrifice a steady paycheck for a while.

<u>Make sure</u> that you have enough money in your bank account to last you a minimum of six months, preferably a year, because in the beginning, all the money you take in from your business will have to go right back into the business. Economize as much as you can. Use coupons. Drive a cheaper car. Cut back on luxuries. Don't eat out, brown bag your lunch. There are perhaps hundreds of ways to cut back (and at least as many books out there to teach you how to do it). So, essentially, you need to be willing to be "poor" for a while. As an entrepreneur, it can be overwhelming in the beginning unless you are prepared for it emotionally as well as financially. So ask yourself, are you prepared?

While this picture may seem bleak to those of you who have never owned your own business, it offers a realistic glimpse at the beginnings of a new venture. When we started our first company in 1995, my husband and I were both working the business and neither one of us was earning a regular paycheck. We were financially overburdened and stressed to the max! Talk about having to cut back on things! It was a little touch and go there for a while, but we learned from this mistake and he went out and worked a "real job" (that included health insurance) while I got the business going. Once the company could afford to pay his salary, he returned to working with me full time.

The lesson here, of course, is this: if you are married to your business partner, make sure that one of you has a steady income coming in as well as health and dental benefits. I also humbly suggest to all married partners out there that they each have their OWN desk, computer and telephone if they value their marriage. Trust me on this one because I am the voice of experience. At one point Ron and I were sharing a desk and computer in the basement of our house. It seemed to be the most cost-effective solution at the time because we could only afford to buy one of everything and sincerely thought that we were capable of sharing.

NOT!

We always needed to use the desk and computer at the same time, and we each thought that our own work was the most important (of course) and should take priority. So we started fighting about it. It drove me crazy!! Soon, however, we found a solution to the problem. We had to separate. Separate our work spaces that is. Once we moved apart, we no longer quibbled about who needed the desk more. Today my office is up on the third floor of our house, and his is on the first floor in the den. We each have a desk, computer, telephone and fax. We don't bicker any more (at least about this issue) and the peace is back. So if you love your spouse then let him/her go ... so to speak.

If you are single, as mentioned before, make it a point to have at least 6 month's salary saved in a readily accessible bank account before you begin. Either way, it is best to work out most of the details that I will be outlining before you quit your current job. Create the framework for your business at night, on weekends, or even by taking a week long vacation to stay at home and work. Once the details are all ironed out, then you can quit your current job and start working on your new business full-time.

Ultimately, my advice can all be boiled down to one old saying that my mother used to say to me --- "Do as I say and not as I do." Just because I made all of these crazy mistakes certainly doesn't mean that you have to.

Now one last thing before we move onto the next chapter. There is a commonly held belief that 80% of new businesses fail in their first five years. This is simply not true! The real statistic comes from the Small Business Administration and reads ...

OF the businesses that fail, 80% do so in the first 5 years.

OF!!!!

That's a far cry different than saying that all businesses fail in the first five years. So when someone quotes that number at you ... turn your ears off.

Here's something else your naysayers might mention to you ...

"How can you start a business now? We're in a recession so it will be impossible to start a business and succeed."

OK ... are we in a recession? Try to get a reservation at a four star restaurant on a Saturday night, or go to an expensive department store and see if you still feel this way. Visit a luxury car dealer and ask them how their sales have been. You'll probably find out everything is fine.

My advice? KNOW THAT YOU CAN DO THIS!! Turn off your ears to the people who tell you that you can't. In fact, when people tell me that I can't do something, it's always inspired me to go out and do it! Been that way all my life.

Change your thoughts and you change your world.

Norman Vincent Peale

Chapter 2

Business Basics

This chapter's purpose is to provide you with a brief overview on how to get your concierge service going. There are many excellent books available that have been written on the subject of starting your own business, so I really don't think it necessary to go into a huge amount of detail here. Several books and websites are listed at the end of each topic where appropriate (as well as at the end of this book). Please remember that these are all only suggestions on how to get your business going. They are all simply ideas that have worked for us.

Company Formation

When forming your company, you have a choice. The following is a breakdown of the different types of companies you can form. I have included the descriptions from the IRS (www.IRS.gov) whenever possible as I can't improve on their definitions and found them to be very clear.

Sole Proprietor

According to the IRS ... "*A sole proprietorship is an unincorporated business that is owned by one individual. It is the simplest form of business organization to start and maintain. The business has no existence apart from you, the owner. Its liabilities are your personal liabilities and you undertake the risks of the business for all assets owned, whether used in the business or personally owned. You include the income and expenses of the business on your own tax return.*"

The pros in this case is that it is easy to organize and there are few legal restrictions. The cons are that you are personally liable for all debts.

Partnership

According to the IRS ... *"A partnership is the relationship existing between two or more persons who join to carry on a trade or business. Each person contributes money, property, labor, or skill, and expects to share in the profits and losses of the business."*

The pros is that it is easy to organize and there are few legal restrictions. The cons is that all partners are personally liable for all debts.

LLC/LLP

Here's a description from the IRS: *"A Limited Liability Company (LLC) is a relatively new business structure allowed by state statute. LLCs are popular because, similar to a corporation, owners have limited personal liability for the debts and actions of the LLC. Other features of LLCs are more like a partnership, providing management flexibility and the benefit of pass-through taxation. Owners of an LLC are called members. Since most states do not restrict ownership, members may include individuals, corporations, other LLCs and foreign entities. There is no maximum number of members. Most states also permit "single member" LLCs, those having only one owner."*

Corporation

According to the IRS ..."*In forming a corporation, prospective shareholders transfer money, property, or both, for the corporation's capital stock. A corporation generally takes the same deductions as a sole proprietorship to compute its taxable income. A corporation can also take special deductions."*

The pros here are that personal assets are not at risk. The cons is that you have double taxation and they are expensive to establish.

S-Corporation

The IRS describes this as *"An eligible domestic corporation can avoid double taxation (once to the shareholders and again to the corporation) by electing to be treated as an S corporation. Generally, an S corporation is exempt from federal income tax other than tax on certain capital gains and passive income."*

The pros here is that you avoid the double taxation and are taxed at the owner's tax rate. The cons are that there is limited liability and you must file additional forms to elect the "S" status.

Employer ID Numbers (EINs)

An Employer Identification Number (EIN), also known as a federal tax identification number, is used to identify a business entity. Everyone needs one. You can apply easily through your accountant, or on-line at: http://www.irs.gov/businesses/small/article/0,,id=102767,00.html.

The information listed above was given to me by my good friend Carla Mandel. Carla is Executive Director of the International Concierge and Errand Association (www.ICEAWeb.org), as well as a great CPA. The rest was obtained from the IRS's website at http://www.irs.gov.

Company Name and Logo

Let's start at the very beginning with your company name. Generally it is wise to choose a name that aptly describes the service that you intend to provide. As a result, words that describe what your service does (like "concierge" or "errand") should probably appear somewhere in your title. Does your area or state have a nickname that people use? In our case we used the word (and symbol) "triangle" because our area is nicknamed "The Triangle."

The logo should start simply. Try using Microsoft Word's "WordArt" or other similar product to give you some ideas. They offer a bunch of different styles that you can use to create your logo. Shapes and symbols are also good to use. If one exists, look into using a symbol/ shape that represents your city.

Legal Issues and Contracts

It would be extremely wise to consult a lawyer <u>before</u> starting your company. He/she will be an excellent resource for you and will assist you in getting incorporated. Be sure the lawyer you choose has experience in business law. A good lawyer can offer practical advice on how to get your business going, what permits and licenses you need and they may even be able to give you the name of a great accountant.

First and foremost <u>you need a contract</u>. The last thing you need is a lawsuit. You should have a member/client contract to protect you from liability issues as well as a simple service vendor agreement stating that you are not responsible for the vendor. Each member should fill out a membership application and sign the contract. Ours is about a page and a half long and is pretty straightforward. Sample contracts may be purchased by going to our bookstore at www.triangleconcierge.com. You can also find service agreements in the contract section of www.entrepreneurmag.com.

We have one contract to cover three separate types of services: individual, corporate and lobby concierge. It includes terms and services, customer responsibilities, compensation and fees, termination, relationship of the parties, warrantees and disclaimers, indemnity by customer, limitation of liability and a miscellaneous section. We have another contract that service vendors are required to sign before we allow them into our business referral service, and we have a third contract for meeting and event planning.

The concierge industry is so young, lawyers do not have any guides or samples to follow when creating a contract for you. So they will be forced to come up with something out of thin air, and they will charge you accordingly. Ours charged us $1,500. So, if you can find another contract for them to just read over (as opposed to creating), then your cost will lower substantially.

No matter whose contracts or agreements you choose to purchase, ***please make sure*** that you have your own lawyer go over it first because each state (and each country) has its own laws and guidelines. Remember, doing it right the first time will avoid any consequences that may pop up. In the long run this will save you a bunch of money.

If you plan on doing any of the meeting or event planning yourself then it is necessary for you to have a contract. This is VERY IMPORTANT! It should outline exactly what you have been hired to do in detail. It should have a basic indemnity clause, act of God clause, cancellation clause, and liability clause. If your client were to cancel the event one week before it is scheduled to occur, what do you do? The hotel will penalize you and you will be out of a great deal of money for the hard work that you've done. Again, a good lawyer can draw a contract up for you if you don't want to use ours.

Meeting Professionals International has some wonderful books on this very subject that can be purchased online from their bookstore at www.mpiweb.org.   Having the appropriate contracts is one of the **most important** parts of setting up this service (the other is insurance). You need someone who can watch your back in case someone sues you. Contracts and insurance will provide this.

If you don't go with a lawyer, call your city municipal building and ask them what the procedure is to incorporate. Also ask them about what permits and licenses you will need to have before you start operating.

So my advice is this ... before you start, find a good lawyer, a great accountant and some good insurance because it is more than worth the time and money. As I said before, doing it right the first time will save you from a great deal of unnecessary hassles.

Accountant

It is also extremely wise to get a good accountant to do your taxes and offer you advice on how to get your books off the ground, how to set up your business, and what resources you will need to purchase. Should your company be an S-corp, an LLC or something else? Your accountant knows the tax laws in your particular area and has the necessary wisdom to advise you properly.

One resource we use is *QuickBooks*, recommended by our own accountant. It is a wonderful product that we use to keep our books, invoices and records. However, if you do not wish to purchase *Quickbooks,* you can use a spreadsheet program like *Microsoft Excel.*

Finally, there is a wonderful webpage where you can purchase all your spreadsheets and forms located at www.villagesoft.com.

Insurance

Everyone needs it and if you're using your spouse's insurance, great! If you're not, then you have to begin shopping around for it. You might also want to give it to your employees as a benefit, once you get employees that is!

[Please note that the following information is not meant to replace what is offered by accredited insurance agencies. It is meant only to be used as a guideline.]

Health Insurance: If you already have insurance because you are on your spouse's insurance plan, this will not apply to you. If you don't and you have to go on Cobra when you quit your job, then by all means keep it for as long as you can. However, once you hire employees (or the Cobra runs out) then you will have to get some health/life insurance. It is best to shop around for the best price. Go directly to the companies themselves to get the best pricing plan for your needs. You might also want to consider dental insurance, which we have found to be very valuable over the years.

Business Insurance: It is not a question of what you think your business is worth, but it is more accurately what you think the largest amount someone could sue you for is. It would be unrealistic to think this could never happen and it is better to be prepared. Business insurance is extremely valuable in the concierge business because of the high amount of liability. To cover yourself, you need business insurance because without it, they can take your personal assets. A good insurance person will be able to guide you in this more thoroughly.

Unfortunately, many of our clients are having a terrible time getting business insurance because not only is the industry only a decade old, but there is no category to put us in. Generally, I suggest to all my clients that they go to an independent insurance broker because they are more "flexible" and can search many companies instead of just one (try several independents).

I also suggest that you tell him/her that they should put you into the "consulting" category or the "janitorial/cleaning house" category.

Bonding each employee will also help. Since one could say that we are similar to a cleaning company in that we both go into people's homes when they are not there, why is there such a problem? The problem lies in the fact that insurance companies are seeing the additional services that a concierge provides ... like errand running in your car or recommending a service vendor (like a deck builder) for example, and other risk management type of tasks that make them think "high liability." It is the liability that the insurance companies worry about.

More to the point, insurance companies don't know who we are and need education on it. They have no idea what a concierge is or what he/she does. You see, insurance is based on codes. This is how they gather their information and develop their risk management policies. Through the codes. Since the concierge business is new, they are unsure as to where to put us because there is no history or code for "concierges," and the history is how they set up their premiums. Insurance companies (like everyone else) want to make money, and unless there is a proven history of good risk management, it is hard to convince them to give coverage.

For more information on concierge insurance, please visit my website at www.triangleconcierge.com and click on "Industry News." There are some companies listed in there that are offering concierge insurance. I post all new information about this topic in there regularly.

Bonds: It is true that you should be able to trust your employees, but according to the U.S. Chamber of Commerce, the fact is that one-third of all employees admitted stealing from their employers during the previous year. Consequently, if you are hiring employees to run errands for you or do some "modified house sitting" (which I will explain in a later chapter) you will have to purchase **Employee Dishonesty Bonds** in addition to your business insurance. These Bonds will protect you from dishonest acts by your employees. It is wise to purchase one bond per employee so that you are fully protected from any theft or embezzlement that may occur.

Lastly, it would be advisable to have each employee sign a simple non-compete clause that your lawyer can draw up for you. You certainly don't want to train your competitors!

One last note ... please **do not** start up your business until you have obtained business liability insurance! I know many concierge out there who are operating without insurance, and it's dangerous. We live in a very litigious society so you need to protect yourself. If you are sued by a client, they'll go after everything they can and you could lose it all.

My advice is to obtain liability insurance, a good lawyer and a great accountant to protect yourself.

You always pass failure on the way to success.

Mickey Rooney

Chapter 3

Your Business Plan

Everyone who starts a new business should have a business plan. Not only will you need one if you plan on obtaining any sort of financing, but it will help organize your thoughts and focus your direction. When writing one you will focus and set your goals and you will identify the problems and pitfalls that you might face. Your business plan should not be long and cumbersome and should clearly outline what your business is, where you plan on going, and how you are going to get there.

There are some wonderful business plan software packages, great websites and numerous books available on the subject. We have listed several good ones in our reference section. Using one of these guides will help you set up your business and make long range plans.

Your business plan should include the following topics:

Chapter I: **Executive Summary**
Introduction
Mission Statement
Unique Features
Marketing Objectives
Expected Accomplishments
Required Capital

Chapter II: **The Business**
                         Problem Statement
                         Description of the Business
                         Founder(s) of the Business
                         Management and Operations
                         Objectives

You will also need to include the financial information described in the pricing section of this book within your business plan. If you need help writing your business plan, a search on the web will prove useful. I found some wonderful companies who were very helpful. Some gave me descriptions of each topic and others gave actual samples. Although you can hire people to write a business plan for you, I would advise against it. There is enough information available for the entrepreneur to save the money for something else.

When I created our business plan I used the *Smart Business Plan Software* (which can be purchased in many stores and mail order companies that carry business software). It is a helpful step-by-step guide that easily helps you to create your own business plan. I suggest that you look at some of the sample plans on www.bplans.com to use as guides and then purchase Business Plan Software to help you write it. It is well worth the price.

There are several parts to a business plan that everyone should include. These sections can be clearly seen in the business plan example found at the end of this book. It provides clear examples of how each section could be written for a concierge company. Please note that these are only examples and are written to provide you with a simple guide when creating your own plan.

Remember, the purpose of a business plan is to provide the reader with a comprehensive synopsis of a business. Therefore we are using the fictional name of "Sample Concierge" as the company name. Please note that this paragraph is to be an introduction to your business and should state exactly what month and year the business started, who started it, where, when business operations will begin and the type of service you want to provide. Since it is the first one people will read, it must capture their interest. It is also the one paragraph that everyone will read thoroughly.

Furthermore, if you are using this plan to obtain capital, then you should state the amount of capital you need in the "required capital" section of your plan. Clearly explain how you will repay the money and the reason why you need the capital. If you are seeking investors, such as venture capitalists, then it is in this section where you should tell them what the return on their investment will be and how long it will take them to get it.

As previously stated, you will find a very simple concierge business plan at the end of this book. Please remember, that this plan is merely included as an example, and serves as a guide for when you sit down to write your own. The numbers are fictitious and only serve as an example of how a table might look. I find that it is always 100% easier to create something new when I have a sample to follow.

People think that at the top there isn't much room.
They tend to think of it as an Everest.
My message is that there is tons of room at the top.

Margaret Thatcher

Chapter 4

Getting Started

Do <u>NOT</u> quit your job, go out and rent an office, buy or rent furniture and hire employees. THINK ABOUT IT FIRST! I'll admit it, I've made that mistake too. We actually did rent an office and purchase furniture with the thought that we would need the office for our future employees. Of course, once everyone knew who we were and what we were doing then our phone would be ringing off the hook, right?

Unfortunately, it didn't happen that way, but it was a nice dream while it lasted. After a while, it dawned on us that the little profit we were making was just going into paying for our monthly overhead. In fact, we were using both our personal savings and our profit to cover the office overhead which, of course, left us with nothing left over to pay for groceries and other necessary items like the mortgage! So we closed our little office and moved the entire operation into our home. The lesson here? Work out of your house until you feel that you can afford an office because in the beginning, you definitely do not want the overhead (or the headaches!).

Instead, convert a small space in your home into an office. You will need a desk, a good computer with a color printer (preferable, but not absolutely necessary) and a fax machine. The best and most cost effective machine to buy us an all in one fax/copier/telephone. Also good to have is a filing cabinet and some office supplies on hand (things like pens, paper, post-it notes, paper clips, stapler, file folders, and the like). Buy a couple of stackable in-boxes because they will help you organize your desk. Organize the boxes into categories like "to be read later," "in," "out," "file" and the like.

You can organize file folders in your filing cabinet in the following categories:

- Accounts payable
- Accounts receivable
- Articles of incorporation
- Audio-visual
- Catalogs
- Computer
- Contracts
- Correspondence
- Entertainment
- Insurance
- Legal
- Local hotels
- Marketing
- Media
- Music
- Out-of-state hotels and resort properties
- Paid bills
- Personnel
- Proposals
- Restaurants
- Service Vendor Contracts and Applications
- Service Vendor Brochures and Information
- Speakers
- Transportation

Organizing your folders now will save time later and as you begin to research your service vendors and meeting/event locations. When a client calls you, you need to have the information at your fingertips so you can get them an answer as quickly as possible.

Finally, it's a good idea to put a second telephone line into your house that you can use for your new business. The second line can double as your fax, modem, and telephone line. In most areas your local telephone company can fix you up with an automatic answering machine so that when your line is busy, the call will automatically be forwarded to your voice mail.

Letterhead and Business Cards

Do yourself a BIG favor and <u>do not</u> go out and buy expensive business cards and letterhead. In the beginning when you have the time, save your money and do it yourself on your computer. Two good products that we use are *Microsoft Publisher* and *Broderbund's Printshop*, although there are many good ones on the market. You could create letterhead in *Microsoft Word* and *Adobe* as well. These software programs include tools that will help you create some really nice business cards, letterhead and brochures for your new business at a reasonable cost. Buy some good 25-pound paper and some nice business card stock and be your own printer until it costs you more in lost time to do it yourself. You can also visit www.vistaprint.com and obtain some affordable business cards.

An ideal business card for an errand/concierge service is the type that folds in half. The outside is your business card with your contact information written clearly. When you open it up it is a micro-brochure with a quick list of some of the services you offer on the inside of it. On the back you could put your picture and a catchy phrase of some sort. (If you have no idea what I'm talking about perhaps this will help ... this type is like two business cards fused together.)

Brochure

When creating your first brochure, look around at what other people have done. Figure out what services you wish to provide and then list them in your brochure. Avoid being too wordy because most people are in a hurry and won't take the time to read a verbose brochure. They are looking for brief, concise overviews outlining the highlights. Save the detailed explanations for your "sales kit." Broderbund's software (mentioned above) includes a really nice wizard that will easily guide you through the brochure process step by step. We have found it to be extremely useful.

What you should include in your brochure:

1. An introduction to your service explaining what a concierge is and what he/she does, as well as what they can do for the individual or corporate entity.
2. A list of services that you provide.
3. A reference list of reputable local businesses you can refer them to.
4. Membership information.
5. Your company name, address, telephone and fax numbers, e-mail address and website address.

Use nice bright colors, borders and graphics to make your brochure attractive and easy to read. Again, look around at other people's brochures to see what aspects appeal to you and implement them into your own brochure. When you are finally ready to get the piece printed, shop around! Go to at least three printers and get the best price. Don't forget that if this printer does a good job for you then you can put them on your service list and refer them out to dozens of people. This is a great incentive for them to not only give you a good price, but to also do a good job so that you will refer them to your clients. Remember, a good marketing piece grabs attention, gives information and, above all, provokes a response of some kind.

The brochure you make should stand out. Get attention and make it as classy and special as possible. Keep the text short and readable in a 10-12 font size (don't use script as it is hard to read). Use bullet copy points to draw interest and make sure you explain how the services will benefit the client. Sell it! Tell them! What problems will it solve? Don't use reverse copy (white words on black) or watermarks as this is also very hard to read. You should also end the brochure with a call to action. CAUSE a response! Use testimonial quotes as they are a very powerful sales tool. Lastly, NEVER mail it just once. Many believe it takes at least 4-5 mailings before someone will respond.

Sales Kit

Your sales kit is also known as your media kit or your press kit depending on what industry we're talking about here. Why do you need one? Well, suppose that you send your brochures out to 1,000 people around town. A few days later you receive a call from someone who has seen your brochure and would like some additional information sent to them. The last thing you want to say to them is that the brochure WAS all your information! You need something else to mail out to them ... hence, the sales kit.

There are many ways you can put this together. You could get some customized folders professionally made up, or you can do it yourself. If you do it yourself, here are some thoughts for you.

First, go out and buy some pocket presentation folders. Then purchase some 1/2 page size labels to put your logo on. Voila! Personalized sales kit folders. Once you begin making the "big" money you can go out to a printer and get some really terrific sales presentation folders made up with your logo on them. For the moment, however, this is the most cost-effective method.

What you should include in your Sales Kit:

1. An introduction/welcome letter.
2. Your biography.
3. Detailed explanations of all the services you intend to provide.
4. Membership (or package) details.
5. Client contract and application.
6. A sheet listing your current rates (subject to change without notice).
7. Your business card.
8. Your company brochure.
9. Your company newsletter.
10. Articles that people/magazines/newspapers have written about you.
11. A reference list of satisfied clients can be added later once you get a few. Be sure to get your clients' permission before you list their name in your kit.

Setting up your databases

You will need a good database like *Microsoft Access* to hold all the information about your clients. You could also go out and purchase ACT. No matter what software you choose, you'll have to keep a database of your members/clients outlining their likes, dislikes, and address. We use *Microsoft Access* because you can design your own database to suit your needs.   Should you indeed opt to do the database yourself, then Microsoft sells a wonderful training CD that will teach you how to use Access. You can usually find the program in your local store next to the Access Software.

No matter what database you decide to use, there is certain information that you will need to know, such as:

- Client's name
- Company name
- Work address
- Home address
- Work phone
- Home phone
- E-mail address
- Spouse name
- Kids
- Interests
- Payment information
- Credit card/check payments
- Notes

As with all the other programs we have mentioned, however, you should shop around for the one that suits your specific needs. I just like *Microsoft Access* because it is so versatile. Each client should receive an ID card with your company name, address, phone number and e-mail address on one side and their company name (if they have one) and ID number on the other. You can save yourself some money and generate these cards from your computer using business card stock and the software program you use for your brochures (such as Microsoft Publisher).

The member/client database might include the following fields:

Customer ID   Birthdate
Member ID   Updated

Prefix

First Name

Last Name

Nickname

Title

Company

Address

City/State/Zip

Home Phone

Work Phone

Email Address

Fax Number

Date

Description of current tasks

Client Status

Hobbies

Health Issues

Marital Status

Spouse Name

Spouse Interests

Children's Names

Acccount Balance

Payment Method

Credit Card Type

Credit Card #

Expiration date

Cardholder Name

Notes

You also might like to design a database for restaurant information. When a client calls and asks you to make a restaurant recommendation for them, you and your staff members need to get the information to the client as soon as possible. This database streamlines the operation so that the information can be at your fingertips as opposed to flipping through the pages of a lengthy restaurant guide.

This database might include the following fields:

- Restaurant ID
- Restaurant Name
- Address
- City
- State
- Zip Code
- Country
- Telephone Number
- Website Address
- Food Type

- Reservations Required? (Yes/No)
- Rating
- Price Range
- Date last updated
- Notes

Lastly, you might want to create two more databases ... a service vendor database and a mailing list database for potential clients. Generally, a company has to see your direct mail piece approximately eight times before they will pick up the telephone and dial your number. The database might include the typical name, address and telephone information that would normally go onto labels or in a personalized form letter.

Once all the databases have been set up you might want to consider networking your computers so that all your employees can have access to the information in the databases (of course, one should probably have employees first!).

If you decide that you do not have the time to do it yourself, then Triangle Concierge sells some very reasonably priced Concierge Software (called *TriTrax PRO*) that has everything you need to get started. It includes databases for client contact information, personal information, vendor database, restaurant database and pertinent financial information. Just log onto our website at www. triangleconcierge.com for all the details.

You can also purchase a database program called ACT. Several of my clients have told me that this software works well for them. Here's their website: http://www.act.com.

Believe in yourself!
Have faith in your abilities!
Without a humble but reasonable confidence in
your own powers you cannot be successful or
happy

Norman Vincent Peale

Chapter 5

Website Creation Made Easy

When it comes to websites you have a number of choices. You can either build a website yourself, you can pay someone to do it or you can utilize templates which build websites for you. At the beginning of our career I considered hiring someone to do it until they quoted me their price. Since we didn't have the revenue to pay for it, I soon abandoned the idea and opted to do it myself with the help of a good friend. It will cost you very little money to do it yourself. If I can teach myself how to do it, so can you!

Once you have the revenue to pay someone else to design a great website for you, then by all means hire someone! Eve-nutallly Ron and I did indeed hire someone to redesign our website. The new site has music, flash and all the bells and whistles. Plus, after they updated the site they turned the files over to me so that I could update the copy on the site as needed.

As my grandmother used to say ... if you have taste you don't need a lot of money. So if you don't have the cash to pay for someone to design one for you, you can do it yourself at half the cost and still have it look great.

One of the benefits of being your own webmaster is that you can make changes quickly and easily from your own com-puter at the exact moment that you think of them. If you hire someone else to maintain your site for you then you will have to forward the changes/additions to him or her. Although it may take you some time to learn, it is well worth it in the end.

E-mail versus URL

For those who are not sure about the difference between e-mail and URL, here are their definitions.

1.   E-mail is a communication tool. Think of it as your telephone number. It is a fast and easy way to communicate with others.

2. URL (Uniform Resource Locator) - think of this as your address. It is a great place for people to find information about both you and your company.

Internet Service Provider

First, before you do anything else you need to get access to the web. Choose a good Internet Service Provider (ISP) like Mindspring, BellSouth, MSN, Roadrunner or Comcast to name a few. What you choose depends on your location and the types of services available. We highly recommend using broadband or DSL because of their high speed. Although they cost a bit more than dial-up, the high speed will save you time and will not test your patience (as much). If you choose (or only have access to) a dial-up provider, then make sure that the provider you choose has several local phone numbers available. There are a lot of companies out there but some are certainly better than others. A good company will offer you Internet access and at least one e-mail account as well as the software you need to get you started. Shop around and find the one that best suits your needs.

Setting up your URL

Your website name can be your company name, or it can be the name of your product and will most likely look like this: www. yourcompanyname.com. Once you choose a name, you must find out if it is available, so you can register the name. Registration fees range from $8.00 to $35.00 a year. You can register it for anywhere from one to ten years. We suggest that you go to www.

register.com, www.networksolutions.com or www.godaddy.com to name a few. There are many out there, these are just to get you started.

If you like, you can also visit the site that we use for our Internet needs. It's actually a nice one-stop shop as it includes getting domain names, hosting, extra emails and helping to register your websites with search engines. Plus you can get a shopping cart if and when you need one. It's the site that we personally use for all our needs and we have found this company to be very cost effective.

Just go to … https://www.securepaynet.net/gdshop/rhp/default.asp?prog_id=triangleconcierge

One more thing, you can have numerous domain names that can be pointed to your website. This is great in situations where someone types in .org or .biz or possibly a business name close to yours as it can generate additional traffic to your website.

Creating the page

Once you have chosen your Internet provider it is time to build your web pages. The software that I use is *Microsoft FrontPage*. It is extremely easy to use and makes very professional looking websites. I know that Microsoft is discontinuiing Frontpage and is now offering three brand-new application building and Web authoring tools. You can see the new products at www http://office.microsoft.com/en-us/assistance/HA101205221033.aspx. If you use another software product (like Dreamweaver for example) that you find better…great! I only listed Microsoft products because they are what I use and make for good examples.

Keep your page as simple as possible because people are generally in a hurry and don't want to spend a lot of time on any one page. Also, remember that you want your page to load quickly so try not to use too many fancy graphics or dark colors. People log onto

your website for the information that it provides, not for the danc-
ing cows.   Keep it clear and easy to read. Bright colors and nice
wallpaper all serve to make your page more attractive. Look around
at other people's websites to get some ideas for your own page.

If you have more than one page then you will have to create a hyperlink to each page. For those who don't know, a hyperlink is a way to
travel from one page or site to another, and it is an easy way to expand
your website. FrontPage does the hyperlinks for you. For example,
on my page (www.triangleconcierge.com) I have a list of contents on
every page so that you never get "lost" within the site and always have
access to the other pages. Each topic is hyperlinked to another page.

Templates

If you don't want to learn another software program, here are some
links to some "instant" website creation sites where you can have a
site up in minutes. Just cut and paste the following codes into your
browser to visit each site.

http://go.bigstep.com/

www.networksolutions.com

There are dozens and dozens of companies out there that will allow you to access their templates and design a site fast. Just do
a search on "create a website" and you'll see dozens come up.

Lastly, here is great little site for templates -

http://www.freesitetemplates.com/

Finding a Web-Hosting company

Now you are ready for a web-hosting company who will host your website. There are a lot of these companies out there so shop around for the best price. A good way to find a hosting company is to do a search on the words "web hosting" and find the one that best suits your needs. Internet providers such as Bellsouth and Mindspring are examples of web hosting companies. You can expect to be charged anywhere from $4.95 a month to hundreds of dollars to host your website, so it just depends on your needs and the size that you require. BEWARE! Know what you are buying! Also remember that you can change hosting companies anytime you want to. Here is a wonderful site that has information about many webhosting companies to help with your decision-making process: http://www.tophosts.com/top25-web-hosts.html

Please do your due diligence and check out what will work for your needs and your budget and do not purchase what you do not need, especially at the beginning. As I've said before, keep it simple!

Web Publishing

OK, now you've chosen your ISP, registered your site, written your page, found a company to host your page and you are set to go. Now it is time to move your page from your own computer to the web. If you are using *Microsoft FrontPage*, then simply click on "publish" and the software will do it all for you. For other programs you can use WS FTP Pro (www.ipswitch.com) to do this and it is available for purchase on the web. It is very simple to use and fast (simple is good for us self-taught people!). Make sure you request the instructions when you download. As with all of these issues, there are plenty of products available both on the Internet, and at your local software supply houses. Simply choose the one that appeals to you.

Someone once told me that a webpage is actually a living and breathing thing and needs to be updated as often as possible to keep it new and fresh. Go to your page at least once a day just to make sure that it is still there and working properly. Once every few weeks add a new page, change something, and update some words...keep working on it. It is like decorating a house...you just never seem to finish it. Remember to add things like newsletters, updates, and new vendors to keep your page fresh.

Search Engines

So you have created your webpage, posted the page and everything seems to work (although I would click on everything just to make sure). Now you have to get people to actually go to the page and read it!

There are a great many ways to do this, but for our purpose let's just keep it simple.

Remember that many search engines will only keep your page up for a certain period of time so you have to re-register your page with the search engines at least once a month. I do it twice a month. It won't take you more than a few minutes or so and is well worth it. I also go to a few of the top search engines myself and simply click on "add a site" which is usually found at the bottom of the page. Some search engines can take up to 8 weeks to add your site, so be patient. Of course, a good webmaster will do this for you, but remember that he/she will also charge you a monthly fee.

Link Exchange

One terrific way to keep in the top ten of the search engines is to exchange links with other companies. Every major search engine uses link analysis as part of their ranking. By building links, you can help improve how well your pages do in link analysis systems. In short, what you really want are links from good web pages that are related to the topics you want to be found for. Here's how to find those good links. Go to the major search engines and do a search on your target keywords. Now go and visit the sites that appear in the top results and email them asking if they would be willing to exchange reciprocal links with you. Now if these websites enjoy a high ranking, then one can assume they're getting a ton of visitors. So if you can get them to exchange links with you then you might pick up some visitors! I've done this with two of my websites and have dramatically increased both the ranking and number of people visiting the site!

One great way to find out how your website is ranked is to get the Alexa Toolbar … here's the link - http://www.alexa.com. I have it on my own computer and think it's great!

Another truly wonderful tool is to visit Virtual Promote at http://www.virtualpromote.com. They have some really terrific articles and tools to help you with your site.

Preparing your site for submission

First, you'll need to write a 25-word or less description of your entire web site … and ideally you should use at least two or three key terms that you hope to be found for within the description. I also suggest that you have a "junk" email address, as search engine submission will generate some additional emails. Personally, I have a Hotmail account that I've set up just for this purpose and I go and clean out the account about once a week. You can use any email address like Hotmail or Yahoo, since they both offer 250 MB of space to handle a lot of emails. Plus they now offer some great SPAM tools.

Although not as important today as it was yesterday, meta tags are still worth it. Do it once and then you never have to do them again! Why use them? Mainly because meta tags offer you the ability to control (to some degree) how your web pages are described by search engines. When you go to a search engine and search for a site, the title of the website and a description of the site pops up. How? The website owner put the title and description in their Meta tags. Ok, I don't pretend to understand any of this, but I do know that it works.

First, here are two articles on meta tags that you can read:

http://searchenginewatch.com/webmasters/article.php/2167931

http://www.philb.com/metatag.htm

I'm going to show you Triangle Concierge's meta tags ... this way you can alter the text a bit and then cut/paste the meta tags into your html code. If you are using *Microsoft FrontPage*, just go to your index page, click on the "html" button on the bottom, and paste the codes on the top. You can also go to the index page and right click your mouse, then type in the description into the dialogue box.

Here are mine:

<TITLE>Triangle Concierge, the Concierge Consultants</TITLE>

<META NAME="keywords" CONTENT="concierge, errand, consultant, corporate concierge, software, training, concierge training, computer, starting an errand service, sales, internet, book, manual, guide, bookstore, seminar, computer software, concierge software, start-up, business services">

<META Name="description" Content="Triangle Concierge is a concierge training and consulting company that provides concierge consulting services to corporations looking to create an in-house concierge department, and to individuals and start-up companies looking to start their own concierge and/or errand service." Description" Triangle>

Submitting the Site

Here are a few search engines where you can submit your site free-of-charge. I would submit to these at least twice a month.

http://www.ineedhits.com/add-it/free/

http://www.google.com/addurl.html

http://dmoz.org/add.html

http://www.alltheweb.com/add_url.php

http://addurl.altavista.com/

http://rex.skyline.net/add/

These engines charge a fee ... but they are well worth it. Paid programs will speed up the listing process and almost certainly generate more search engine related traffic for your web site.

www.lycos.com

www.yahoo.com

http://ask.ineedhits.com/

Now here's what Ron and I think works the best. Pay-per-Click! It's the best way to get people to your website because you have CON-TROL and SUCCESS. The two pay-per-click sites that we use are http://www.overture.com and www.adwords.com. You pay a small fee (5 to 10 Cents or higher per click) for every click you get, and you set the price that you would like to pay. Of course, the higher the fee, the higher and sooner your website can be found and clicked on.

Lastly, here are a few links to some GREAT websites and articles that will provide you with a lot more information on this topic.

http://www.searchenginewatch.com

http://selfpromotion.com

http://www.wisecat.verywise.co.uk/search-engines.htm

It is also a good idea to advertise your website absolutely every-where...on your answering machine, business cards, letterhead, company brochure, correspondence and even on the magnetic sign on your car!

Here are a few more tips that you should definitely know about ...

Do not ever send emails to people for marketing purpose without their approval to do so. This is considered SPAM and you can lose your access to the Internet because of it. Use tools to block SPAM, Spy Ware to protect privacy and Virus Protection to protect your computer and your files. In fact, you can download FREE software at www.download.com that can help protect your computer and your privacy. If you need to research computers and other gadgets, just go to www.cnet.com.

Lastly, a little advice ... since about 80% of your traffic will come from the top 15-20 search engines, don't waste your money on those companies that tell you they'll submit your site to over 1000 engines. We did that once and our ranking actually went down instead of up. If you decide to take this course, I would still submit to search engines myself just to make sure the site is getting submitted. I would also visit the top search engines once in a while so that you can stay on top of where you are in the engine.

Now please note ... the minute I finished that last paragraph it became obsolete. The computer world is changing so fast it's hard to keep up, but this chapter should at least give you the basics.

Chapter 6

Setting up your Services

As good workers become increasingly hard to find, businesses are looking for new and effective ways to either attract or retain valuable employees. According to *Good Morning America* "absentee-ism has tripled in the workplace in the last year due to stress." Concierge services alleviate some of that stress because they take some of the day-to-day tasks off their client's shoulders. They create some additional time for employees to relax.

Companies around the nation will now be able to offer employees a host of services to help alleviate some of that stress — from picking up dry cleaning, running errands and managing catered business lunches to personal shopping, business referrals, ordering dinner and shopping for clothes. Instead of making 20 calls, the employee has to make only one.

There are many different ways to set up a concierge service. Some companies provide all of the following services, and others concentrate on only one. I think that it is important for you to understand how concierge companies in general set up their service so that you have a "sample" of sorts to follow when we begin to discuss your new service. Therefore, below is an overview of the various ways concierge companies set up their companies and the services that they provide.

It's All About the Money

It's all about the money right? Giving or receiving, this seems to be everyone's focus right now. It also happens to be the number one topic that I get asked by my clients. So I've decided to write about it to answer some of the questions that I've been getting recently.

First, I think a little history about money would be in order. My good friend Connie Domino sums it up perfectly in her book *Develop Irresistible Attraction* ...

> "As a consequence of the Renaissance, the Protestant Reformation, and the Enlightenment, the West (including our society) began to organize itself around trade, commerce, scientific achievement, and a more democratic government. All this makes money a key ingredient. This was not necessarily a bad thing and was certainly a step in the right direction as it was away from a society organized around a government run by aristocracy, or by officials of a certain religion. If you ever visit a very diverse city such as New York City, you will notice that people of different ethnic backgrounds, religions, political beliefs, etc. can live peacefully side by side when their larger society is organized around trade and commerce. This shapes their interactions with one another as ones of economic interdependence and respect for each other's contributions. However, the moment the larger society and government becomes organized around one religion over another, or one social class over another, then all kinds of trouble begins. No one can agree which religion the government should represent, or which social class should be 'tops.'

While organizing a society around trade and commerce can quell many political and religious squabbles amongst diverse groups of people, it can lead to a type of materialist view of the world. Also, the theocracies, and monarchies (claiming the divine right of kings) that many of the world's people lived under for years, taught them that money was bad and indeed the 'root of all evil.' I believe this was taught to the masses to keep them from revolting against the people in power who also happened to be the people with all the money. These negative teachings about money followed the people down through the ages and right into today.

This history of how people have been taught to think and feel about money has created quite a dichotomy in their experience with it. As a result, many people have developed a kind of love/hate relationship with money. 'I love money, but it is bad. I need money, but it may make me a bad person.' When a person can't become clear in their head and heart about money, their wishes for money just bounce around the universe, and they do not consistency manifest what they truly desire. Many traditional religions also taught that 'money is the root of all evil, life is suppose to be hard, and we are supposed to suffer.' The result of all this negative programming is that many of us grew up thinking we simply don't 'deserve' great prosperity in our lives.

We must become conscious and clear regarding our thoughts and feelings about money, before we can consistency manifest it. Money, just like anything else, is made of energy. The paper, ink and coins themselves are made of the same energy as in any other material object. What money represents as a medium of trade is also a type of energy placed into motion. Money is no more or no less than a medium for the exchange of energy. Therefore, there is absolutely no reason to get all caught up in confused feelings about money."

About the Author - Quoted from Connie Domino's book: *Develop Irresistible Attraction. In 5 easy steps - Meet your life goals and desires in as little as 2 weeks using The Law of Attraction.* Available at www.ConnieDomino.com

Besides Connie's great book, I've been reading a lot of other books on this particular topic. Not because I have a lot of time to kill (*I wish!*), but more because I finally decided that if I wanted to BE prosperous then perhaps it was time to THINK prosperous. Knowing that you can be prosperous and that you DESERVE it is the first step to success. Now knowing and doing are two very different things. I can know that I want to be prosperous, but actually doing it is harder.I know with me I had to change my thinking around if I wanted to attain any prosperity at all. So after a little soul searching I discovered that deep down I didn't think I deserved to be prosperous.

Wow ... that was a revelation! I also discovered that I didn't like money. I had the misguided thought that money was the root of all evil, and would turn you into a sort of Frankenstein consumed with greed if you had too much of it. Hmmm ... sounds like a bad movie.

The good news is that eventually I decided that it was time to get rid of those nasty little thoughts and change my ideas on the subject. How did I do it? I started visualizing my perfect life ... I daydreamed about my books being successful, I visualized my company being successful, I saw myself speaking to large groups of people and I imagined that all my bills were paid with money left over in the bank. Then I wrote down goals to get me there. Miraculously at some point along the way, my entire paradigm changed and the old thoughts slipped away forever.

What I've learned from this is that fear is a life-changing thought that can propel you into a direction that you don't want to go. It's like a runaway train that you are incapable of stopping and can't jump off. It consumes you until you can't think of anything else. In my case it was fear of both having money and not having it. It was crazy!! It was the fear of bankruptcy, fear of losing my house and the fear of losing everything I hold dear. On the other hand, it was also the unreasonable fear that actually having money would turn me into a horrible ego-filled greedy person. This irrational fear controlled my thoughts and my actions and propelled me onto a path that was as far from prosperity that you could get. It was all I could think about and I worried about it constantly. In fact, it was my entire focus for years. I was indeed on a runaway train and I didn't think there was any way to stop it … but there was. I eventually did jump off the train and started walking down a new road. I am now embracing prosperity instead of rejecting it and know that not only will my goals and dreams come true, but I'll now be able to pass it forward.

You too can jump off your train … you can change your life and reach your dream. Just have faith and you can do anything!! Remember that prosperity doesn't necessarily mean having as much money as possible. For me, prosperity is having the means to help as many people as possible … and still be able to pay my bills. Prosperity means being able to give it away.

What is the true meaning of prosperity? Having the means to be able to pass it forward and help someone else attain their dream.

How to set your Fees

Figuring out how much to charge is probably the most difficult part of starting up any business. It is especially hard in this business because the industry is so young and as a result there are no real guidelines to follow. The US Anti-Trust Act tells me that I cannot tell you what to charge, but I can certainly help you figure it out. Every market is different so fees are set according to a number of factors ... region, overhead and who you are marketing to.

Region - Since the cost of living (or the average salary of the area) varies from region to region, so do the fees. The fee I might charge someone living in New York City or Los Angeles, for example, will be different from the fee I might charge someone living in North Carolina or Utah.

Who are you marketing to? What are people willing to pay for your services in your area? Are you going after blue-collar workers or white-collar, the city or the suburbs, upper or middle class?

The fees that you might charge to the middle class market will be very different from those you would charge to the upper class. In other words, the price I would charge a middle class worker who earns a salary of five figures per year, for example, would be very different from the price I might charge an affluent-type person who earns a salary in the six and seven figure range.

Overhead - It is helpful to establish four things before you set your fees so that you know where you need to be financially and where you would like to go in the future. (You will also need all of these numbers for your business plan).

1.   Overhead
2.   Percentage you are going to spend towards marketing
3.   Your daily labor rate
4.   Profit

Establishing your Daily Labor Rate

First you need to decide on the yearly amount that you are worth. For example, suppose you decide that you are worth $40,000 per year ...

1. $40,000 per year
2.   Divided by 261 work days *(this takes into account weekends, vacation days, sick days and holidays)*
3.   Total would be $153.26
4.   Your daily labor rate in this case would be $153.26 (*not including overhead*).

Now I know that all of you out there want to earn a six-figure income or more. However, we have to start somewhere. If you love math, then using the formula above will help you figure out what you would like to charge hourly. If you don't like math (like me) keep reading, as I have some non-math ways to figure this out.

Establishing Overhead

Overhead covers your fixed expenses including: office rent, salary, office furniture, supplies, telephone bill, company credit cards, accountant fees and marketing. Of course as your business expands, so will your overhead. The trick is to keep it manageable!

The following is a partial list of what your overhead might be:

- Office rent
- Telephone
- Office supplies
- Rental of office furniture
- Postage
- Insurance
- Accountant fees
- Legal fees
- Printing
- Photocopying
- Personnel salary and benefits
- Dues and magazine subscriptions
- Memberships
- Marketing
- Business licenses and taxes

Let me elaborate on a few items on the list…

Office Rent: Don't go out and rent an office until you have regular clients. Work out of your home until you get some clients and employees and need the additional space. Shop around for the best price and only rent what you need. A simple two or three room office should suffice in the beginning.

Telephone, Office Supplies, Rental of Office Furniture and more: Everyone knows it is always best to shop around for the best price and it is no different here. From office supplies to telephone…shop around. Spend wisely, and save your receipts. If you need furniture, look in the newspaper for companies who are selling theirs as you might be able to pick up some great stuff for low prices.

You can find some very tasteful furniture at bargain prices by going through the newspaper and second-hand shops (we did and I'll venture a wager that you would never know it if you came to my office). You should also consider renting your furniture since sometimes rental companies have some great packages!

Insurance, Accountant Fees, Legal Fees: I can't stress this enough... do it right the first time. Call your insurance agent, lawyer and accountant BEFORE you open for business and consult with them on what you need to do. Show them the sample contracts, talk about your business plan and buy some insurance - it is more than worth it!

Printing, Photocopying: It is not necessary to rent an expensive copy machine in the beginning, just go out and buy a copier/fax/telephone all in one machine. It will do the small jobs for you. The large jobs can be done outside the office at stores like Staples, Office Max, Office Depot or a commercial printer. As always, shop around for the best price. The good news here is that you might be able to get these people to become a "service vendor" and in which case you will earn a commission for each job you bring them. Once you get your business up and running, you can rent a really good copier and do some of the smaller printing jobs yourself. Then, instead of paying a printer the per copy charge you can keep it for yourself. A lot of companies do this and it can be quite lucrative.

Personnel salary and benefits: If you have staff, you will have to give them benefits (like medical and dental insurance). There are many options available in today's competitive market. Make sure you also give an employee handbook to each staff member that clearly states your policies. You can find an example of one at the end of this book.

Break Even Point: You reach your break even point when your expenses (including the money you invested into the business and/or loans) match your revenue. In other words, take all your expenses and overhead including all salaries, benefits and office/operation expenses, and match it with the revenue that is generated by the company. You are considered a profitable company once you have reached your breakeven point and you get out of the red. Also, you should keep excellent records for all expenses that your business generates. These include all office expenses, travel, entertainment, marketing materials and the like. If you spent it on your business to get business then it is an expense.

You also might be considering paying yourself a salary (or any partners that you might have). Whether or not this is a good idea really depends on how you would like to structure your company and the amount of revenue that you are generating. Also it would depend on the type of company you create (such as corporation, partnership, etc) and the best tax advantages to each, which you should of course discuss with your lawyer and accountant.

It might take a year or it might take a few years to show a profit. Revenue is the key to your growth and success! Continuing to grow your revenue and finding ways to cut expenses without hurting your business and slowing its growth are the keys to profitability.

So our advice is this ... grow your business while keeping your expenses down. Try and not spend your money on unnecessary things (like expensive advertising, for example, or expensive letterhead and business cards). Make careful investments into your business as your company grows.

Fees - How much do I charge?

Fee setting is actually one of the elements of marketing your service because it tells people that you are going to give them quality services for their money. A low fee may bring you clients initially, but it might not be enough to sustain your business. You can also set a "rack rate" type of fee so that it allows you to offer your members/ clients a discounted rate or better yet a preferred rate. A rack rate being the highest rate that you would charge for a particular service and discounted/preferred rate is what a client could be charge for particular type or services or amount of services provided.

Hotels will offer their sleeping room rack rates to people who walk in off the street. You can obtain a discount for the sleeping room if you have a AAA card, AARP card or a meeting planner has negotiated a special rate for you. The same can be said for your concierge services. Remember folks, you can always come down from an advertised price, it's hard to go up. Do not set rates that are high and unreasonable, instead you should set for the high end of the market rate. You do not want to scare away potential clients.

You might even want to consider conducting some market research in your area to find out what people might consider paying for a service like yours. Give them a range of choices and see what they say! Call family, friends, and acquaintances and just ask. The information you get back will be invaluable.

When setting your fees ... you can put them into two categories ...

Concierge/ Lifestyle Management Services - These are any services that can be done from the comfort of your desk via telephone, fax, e-mail and the Internet.

Personal Assistant Services - Also called errand services, these are services that require you to leave your desk, get into your car and go out and do something for someone.

Now in today's market, there are two basic ways to set up your fees.

Membership Style - Also known as "Packages"

Concierge companies who set up the fees in this style generally charge a yearly membership fee (which could also be a retainer fee) plus fees for other services.

I have seen membership fees range from $75 to $750 to $5,000 to $10,000 and more per year depending on their location. In other words, companies located in New York City and Los Angeles would charge on the "high" end, and other companies in places in smaller tiered cities like Des Moines, Iowa, for example, would charge on the low-medium end. On top of the membership fee, companies charge the client (usually on an hourly basis) for many other services such as meeting and event planning, errand running, personal shopping and researching for a product or a service. Hourly rates also vary depending on the type and location of the service.

The yearly fee usually comes with some complimentary services such as a certain number of errand service hours, business referral services, travel and vacation services and the like. Many companies offer several packages (or memberships) so they can meet every one's budget.

Here's an example of how you might figure out your monthly retainer fee. Please remember that this is only an example. I know companies who charge three, four and even five figure numbers. Anything goes here! It also depends on who your target market is and what the cost of living in your area is. There are dozens of ways to figure this out. Remember, the numbers below are only an example.

Now let's assume that an average client will use the service 5 hours per month, and we'll say that you charge $25 per hour for your services.

$$5 \times \$25 = \$125$$
$$\$125 \times 12 \text{ months} = \$1,500$$

You might then add an hour or two onto this number to account for the concierge service calls that you might get from the client. Remember, one phone call will take about 5 minutes. So you could potentially make quite a few calls in one hour.

$$2 \text{ hours} \times \$25 = 50$$
$$\$50 \times 12 \text{ months} = \$600$$

Your top membership package could then be $2,100 per year and would include "free" things (services) such as …

Unlimited Concierge Service Calls
Up to 5 hours per month personal assistant service
Travel and vacation service
Business referral service
Restaurant reservations

Remember, the more times they call you for something, the more chances you have to make money in commissions from outsourcing the work to another vendor, or from doing the work yourself. Plus, these are your TOP clients, so I think this particular package has to be great. You could add more money onto it if you like to cover the cost of the concierge service part. Perhaps a few hundred dollars. The next package, of course, would cost less and might include a few different things.

If you do decide to charge a yearly membership fee, it generally does <u>NOT</u> include other services like meeting/event planning, errand services, or personal shopping. As I stated earlier, many concierge companies will give their clients a few complimentary errand/personal shopping hours along with the membership, as well as a myriad of other "free" services. Other companies will limit how many times your clients can call in per week. Many other companies do not limit the amount of times a client can call because the company generally gets a commission or a fee every time they do.

Lastly, instead of packages, some companies are now selling blocks of time. For example, they would sell you 10 hours of time giving you one or two hours for free (you would only pay for 8 or 9). You can then use these hours any time you want with no restrictions.

Restaurant Style or A La Carte

The other way to set up your service is "restaurant style." This means that you provide your client with a menu of services with no membership fee. It is a "pay as you go" service. These companies also sell various products to their clients. A detailed breakdown of all the services along with their costs is usually quoted to the client. For example, the quote would include rates for errand and personal shopping service, meeting/event planning, and a special date reminder service.

Let me tell you what the market generally bears.

For errands, I have seen charges ranging from $12 to $75 (and higher!)

per hour. It really depends on the location and the logistics. Meeting and event planning hourly rates range from $50-200 per hour. Things like personal shopping and doing errands like waiting for the cable repairman are all charged hourly. Based on my research, and on the research recently put out by the International Concierge and Errand Association (www.ICEAWeb.org), the average hourly rate for concierge and errand services in the United States seems to falling between $25-65 per hour.

Some companies are offering Prepaid Gift-Certificates. Others have clients pay for blocks of time. For example, a one hour block could be $18 per hour; 5-hour block is $17 per hour and so on.

Now there are three basic forms of concierge services ...

Individual Concierge Services

This service is for everyone. It is the perfect gift for the holidays (or any other occasion) for anyone who is overworked, stressed out, and needs a little helping hand once in a while. Individual members are charged either a yearly membership fee or can choose to be charged on an "as they go" basis. Clients may fax, e-mail or telephone their requests as often as they wish. Of course, there are companies who limit the number of requests their clients can make on a per week basis. For example, some companies allow you 2-3 calls per week. Other companies allow unlimited requests.

Corporate Concierge Service

This is designed for those companies who request services to be provided remotely via telephone, fax or e-mail. The cost can easily be made a part of either the company's employee benefits package or as a payroll deduction. Employees enjoy this service because it allows them to spend more time with their families, and their employers enjoy this service because it keeps the employees at their desks longer, where they are more focused and can concentrate on the tasks at hand. A true win-win situation!

Once the contract is signed making you the company's exclusive concierge company, you should send each employee/client a welcome packet of information about your company. This might include a list of all the services that you provide, rate information, and coupons for complimentary services. You actually want them to call as often as they can because the more they call, the more money you make in commissions from your service vendors. It is also a nice touch to mail your clients a monthly newsletter outlining new services, giving them coupons to use and providing them with other useful information. Doing this keeps your name in front of them as a reminder to use your service.

Each client should fill out a client application when they use your services so that you can provide them with the best service possible. A sample application can be found at the back of this book. Quite often you will take their information over the phone when they call you whether they are corporate or individual clients. Lobby concierges will get the information in person since the client is usually standing right in front of them.

You should try and provide personal service to everyone, so the more information you can get, the more services you can provide to them that are geared towards their likes and dislikes and personal situation. Their specific requests are logged into the computer so you can remember them for the next time they call. And since personal service is the hallmark of the concierge service, your client's privacy is something that should be guaranteed. Assure your clients that you will never sell your client's name lists to outside vendors. In this type of business, it is critical that your clients trust you.

There are dozens of ways to set this up. Here are two examples ...

Monthly Fee

Like the membership fee idea mentioned earlier, this can also be called a retainer fee, you can charge the company one price per employee per year to retain your services. This fee can be paid monthly, quarterly, bi-annually or yearly. Each employee is responsible for paying for your services. Services might include concierge services, personal assistant or errand services, meeting planning and personal shopping.

Companies today are making concierge services a part of their corporate benefits package which increases their employee retention rate. Further, as employees become less stressed out they will take less and less sick and personal days and their overall health and wellness will increase thus lowering their insurance premiums ... which directly affects the company's bottom line. It will also give them an edge on their competition. Finally, it will add another benefit to each employee's package at little (or no) cost to the employer.

Flat Fee

On the other hand, some of my clients charge the company a flat fee per year, plus the cost of the errands. One way to figure out this rate is to take your hourly rate (let's say $20) and multiply that $20 by the number of employees. If that number is simply too high then you can try wording it this way ... ABC Company has 500 employees. Using our formula, you might charge them a yearly fee of $10,000, which boils down to only $27 per day. If this just seems to darn high, then half it and charge them $5,000.

According to my own research over the years, approximately 10% of the employees will use your service in the first 3 months or so. After that the number might go up to 45% or so. I highly doubt that you'll ever get all the employees in a company to use this service. Now I can wrap my brain around 10% of a 1000 person company better than I can the whole number. It becomes more manageable.

I also suggest that you tell the company that it will take at least four to six weeks to set up their service. This will give you plenty of time to hire a staff and set everything up.

On-Site/Lobby Concierge Service

If you are setting up an On-Site (or lobby) Concierge business then I would suggest costing out exactly what the monthly overhead will be. Overhead such as salary for the person manning the desk, a desk or kiosk, several chairs, telephone, computer, and supplies (of course if the client supplies their own desk and chairs, the cost goes down). Add a small profit onto the number. Remember, you are not looking to make a huge profit on the real estate management companies, you just want to break even and cover your costs. In fact, what you actually want is access to all the employees in the building so they can use your service. As the tenants use your new service and take advantage of your wonderful vendors, your revenue will substantially increase. Not only do you obtain revenue from the errand service charges, but each service vendor will pay you a commission.

The profit here is in the commissions and errand services. The more dry cleaning you take to your official dry cleaner (many cleaners will give you a commission on the cleaning that you bring to them), the more errands you run, and the more business referrals that you give out, the more money you make. It is for this reason that you should consider offering your lobby concierges a salary and commission based on the number of sales they do. It is a basic sales strategy, the more revenue generated by the on-site concierge, the larger his/her income will be. Therefore, incentives (such as bonuses) are a wonderful way to get them to increase their sales.

Dru Jensen Jones, who used to run Concierge Concepts International in Jacksonville, Florida calculated the monthly fee by the following formula. Other companies calculate costs by square footage. There are hundreds of ways to figure this one out!

Here's the formula that Dru uses ...

1. Take the number of units in the building and multiply that by 2 people, on average, per unit.

2. 35% of that total number is the percentage of residents that will typically utilize the service consistently.

3. Multiply that number by 6 requests per month (average of number of requests currently receiving—average.)

4. Multiply that number by the 12-15 minutes it take to facilitate a request and then divide by 60 minutes (1 hour). This equals the number of hours per month that they technically would need to have covered to provide services for that number of people

5. Multiply your hourly rate by the number of hours calculated and this equals the monthly fee for one person to provide service on a regular 9-5, 5-day/week engagement.

EXAMPLE: for a 250 unit-condo ...

• 250 x 2 people per unit = 500 people

• 35% of 500 people is 175 people that could potentially utilize the service consistently

• 175 people averaging 6 requests (probably less for a new, developing property) per month = 1050 potential requests per month

• 1050 requests x 12 minutes for execution = 12,600 minutes divided by 60 minutes = 210 hours per month in service request execution

• 210 x $25/hr = $5,250.00 for the monthly service rate. $5,250.00 x 12 = $63,000 (Annual Contract Amount less Management Fee)

Some people add in a Management Fee (monthly profit) equivalent to one month's service fee or an amount of your choosing, that is due in addition to the monthly service fee.

The above formula can also be used to calculate the retainer fee for a corporation. In the example used, instead of a 250 unit condo, it would be a 500-person corporation.

Now please remember, the $5,250 you receive per month is not what gets deposited as profit into your bank account. The money pays for your overhead to do the job.

Here's the non-math way of figuring it all out. Ideally, you really just want your overhead covered. Perhaps your client needs a 7-day/week service, which will require a full-time weekly concierge and a part-time weekend concierge. To determine the monthly rate, figure out the monthly payroll costs per person, then add-in your overhead (payroll taxes, administrative fees, insurance, tax/liability, overhead, bonding, training, furniture rental, etc.). Then you can add a 10-15% profit or assess an annual management fee at your discretion. I'm pretty sure the number you arrive at will be very similar to the one you'll get using the math formula.

This service can be done part-time, full-time or remotely (via telephone, fax or email) depending on the needs of the client.

How is the client going to pay for the services?

Good question. I suggest that you make your service a pre-paid one.

By creating the concierge account, you are creating a pre-paid service. Clients know right from the start that everything must be paid for in advance with either their credit card, personal check, or the money currently in their concierge account.

What if you go out and purchase $75 worth of groceries for a client, and when your errand driver gets to the house the spouse answers the door and refuses delivery? All of sudden you're stuck with $75 worth of groceries! A pre-paid service solves this problem from the outset.

If you wish to accept credit cards, you can set that up in a few ways. You can use *PayPal* at www.paypal.com, or you can create a merchant account. The easiest way to do this is to go through *Quickbooks* - an accounting software that is awesome!! A must-have for every entrepreneur and very user-friendly. You can set up everything through it. You can also go to your bank and obtain a merchant account with them if you like.

Concierge Accounts

Another way our clients are setting their fee structure up is by creating *concierge accounts* for each client. Here's how it works - the
client puts a set amount of money into the concierge account such
as $50, $100, $250 for example. Then you draw your hourly rate,
plus the cost of the actual services from their account. When the account starts to get low, you just call them up and ask if they would
like to deposit more money into their account. The actual money
they give to you should be placed in your own company checking account. Then, you keep track of their account using your accounting software (such as *Quickbooks*), *TriTrax PRO* or a ledger.

Concierge Accounts are an ideal way to set up clients who might not
have credit cards and would like to keep some money in their account.
A great solution to get clients to pre-pay for your service!!

Services You Can Offer

Other services are often provided as well. Several companies I know
of specialize in errand and personal shopping services. Another
company specializes in tickets, dinner reservations and finding the
"hard to find" items. Yet another company specializes in the senior
citizen market and delivers groceries and runs errands. Here are a
few ideas:

Errand Service/Personal Shopping

You can set up an errand service and do your client's errands for them.
Errands might inlcude running to the post office, picking up dry

cleaning, going to the grocery store, hardware store, pet services, senior care, modified house sitting or picking up a gift at the mall. Anything goes here and it can be very lucrative. Figure that you can run at least 3-5 errands per hour, depending on what they are and their proximity to each other. You pay someone $8-15 per hour to run the errands for you (the rates really depends on the location) and you charge the client anywhere from $15-30 per hour (or you charge per errand) to run the errand. You can offer several "free" errand hours as an incentive to try the service. The client gets their errands done and the company makes a nice profit. This may not seem like a lot of money, but it adds up quickly. The trick is getting your clients to try the service.

One word of caution. Please be very careful if you purchase liquor for a client. At the very least, please make sure that the person you are delivering to is over 21. I would also check your state laws, as several states have set rules about transporting alcohol. I would also check with your lawyer about this issue.

Business Referral Service

This is a wonderful service that you can offer your clients. Once you have done the legwork, there is no additional cost involved and you can offer it for free. Some other concierge services charge the vendor a yearly fee to participate in the service. For others, vendors give a 10-15% commission on any business that results in a sale and the client gets the referral they need. Everyone needs a painter, electrician, plumber, insurance agent, or realtor from time to time, but you can't always be sure that you're getting the best when you randomly pick someone out of the Yellow Pages. You should personally interview each service provider, call their references, and have them sign a contract, thus ensuring a quality contact for your clients. Of course, if they don't comply with your agreement then you might wish to drop them immediately and replace them with a competitor. You are offering first-class service to your clients, and if your vendors can't provide first-class service, then they should be replaced with someone who can.

Senior Assistance/Sick Care

There are so many senior citizens out there who are not quite ready for a home, but yet still need some assistance. They need someone to buy their groceries and stock their refrigerator, pick up their prescriptions, walk/feed their dog or cat, tidy up the house and the like. Most of the time their adult children help out with the daily tasks. Children with families of their own to take care of! In comes the concierge to the rescue. All of these "to do's" can be done by a reputable concierge who can even call the adult child and tell them "I'm here and your mom is fine." How to market this? Not to the seniors because most do not have a dime to spare. Market instead to the adult children who need an extra helping hand in balancing their complicated lives.

Even More Services

Pet care
Personal chef services
Obtaining Tickets to concerts, sporting events, etc...
Auto maintenance
Home organization
Travel/vacation planning
Obtaining promotional materials (pens, coffee mugs, etc.)
Internet research
Employee relocation services
Corporate housing
Corporate gifts
Find a child a tutor

Traveling notary services
Bill payments
Cleaning Services
Courier/delivery service
Dining reservations
Gift baskets
Flower delivery
Dry cleaning services
Landscape services
Meal delivery
Merchandise returns
Mystery shopping
Repair/service calls
Special day reminders
Senior care services
New mommy services

Remember ... these are just a few of the services you can provide! The list is really quite endless. The real list can be found in the Yellow Pages.

In short, concierge will do anything as long as it's legal, ethical and moral.

The greatest mistake you can make
is to be continually fearing you will make one.

Elbert Hubbard

Chapter 7

Meeting and Event Planning

If you are planning on outsourcing your meetings/events, then please skip this section and go directly to chapter 8 on page 115. If not, then read on!

There is so much involved in meeting and event planning that the topic could take its own book to fully describe. However, in the interests of time and space this chapter will only briefly discuss the major details. If you wish to learn more about this topic check the resource library on the webpage of Meeting Professionals International at www.mpiweb.org. There are some really excellent guides available to help you prepare for meeting planning.

Potential scenario: A client calls your office requesting help planning their daughter's wedding. A few minutes later a second client calls asking for help planning their annual holiday party and a third client wants to have a meeting for some out-of-town clients.

In this industry, you have three very distinct choices here:

1. You call an independent meeting/event planner and farm the events out to them. Meeting planners generally charge anywhere from $50 -$250 per hour for their services, and you should receive a 10% commission on the total price charged to the client.

2. You farm out one or two of the events to the independent meeting planner and you do the third one yourself.

3. You do all of the events yourself and keep the fee.

The most lucrative choice, of course, would be to do everything yourself. However, if you have never planned a meeting in your life, the task can be daunting. Here are a few simple tips that will make your life easier. For further information, check out the library at Meeting Professionals International www.mpiweb.org. Each of the following topics is discussed in detail with a complete list of resources. This list is only intended to help you get started.

Budgets and Clients - getting started

The first thing you need to do is to obtain some basic information from the client:

1. What kind of function is it? Birthday, wedding, anniversary, company picnic, office party, seminar, meeting, networking reception, or exhibit?

2. How much do they want to spend? Obtain a budget for the event.

3. How many people will be there?

4. When do they want to have it - date and time of the event?

5. Where do they want to have it? Hotel, restaurant, convention center?

6. Do they want it centered around a theme of some kind, a company logo, a specific season or perhaps even a specific color?

7. Do they need entertainment? If yes, what kind?

8. Is it a food function? If yes, sit-down or buffet? Full meal or hors d'oeuvres?

9. Will invitations need to be sent out? If yes, do they want help?

10. Will they need flowers, decorations or a photographer?

Once the client furnishes you with this information, you can begin to find a location for the event.

Site Selection — How to find the site

Once I have obtained the preliminary information from my client, I gather together a list of properties that I think would work for them. Then I call each property to check for availability. If the site is available, I make an appointment with the sales manager to tour the property and discuss the upcoming event.

I have a rule that has served me well during the 15 years I have been a meeting planner. You never book a property without seeing it first!

Always do a site inspection of the property before you suggest it or sign any contracts because you need to know if the location will work for your client. Taking a few of your own photographs can also be helpful if clients are unable to visit the location for themselves.

How do I find the properties? Both your local Chamber of Commerce and your Convention and Visitors Bureau (CV&B) will be able to help you. If you give your local CV&B the details of the event they will find some properties for you — FREE! This is a truly valuable resource and one I use frequently. The Yellow Pages can also be useful by looking under topics such as hotels, motels, conventions and restaurants. Valuable listings can also be found on the Internet by conducting a search through your local city. Once at the site, there are several key things that I look for.

1. Is it clean, neat and orderly? Nicely decorated? Did someone greet you when you arrived?

2. Is the meeting room or event space large enough for your group? Is it nicely furnished?

3. Where is the kitchen? If it's on another floor the food might be cold by the time it arrives. Also if the kitchen is directly on the other side of the room you're meeting in, be careful. I once booked a meeting in NYC in a really nice hotel only to find the kitchen was just on the other side of the wall. All during the meeting you could hear dishes rattling, carts rolling around, people talking – it was very disruptive.

4. Do they have an in-house audio-visual department or will you have to hire one outside?

5. Where are the bathrooms and how many are there? I'm not kidding about this one. I know someone who once booked a meeting for 1,000 people and forgot to check this. Once there, she found out that there was one ladies room with only three stalls! You can only imagine what happened!

6. Are there telephones nearby? How many? Where are they?

7. For a hotel, what about the sleeping rooms? Are they nicely furnished? How large are they? Are they clean? Is the rug clean? Bathroom? What kinds of amenities come with it? Hair dryers, irons and ironing boards? Can a person hook up their laptop?

8.   If some of your client's guests will be coming from out-of town, you need to find out how far the property is from the airport and public transportation. Do they have a shuttle?

9.   Ask the salesperson when they plan on updating, or redecorating the property. The last thing you want is your people to be greeted by a construction site!

10. What type of deposit do they require? What is their cancellation policy?

11. Are there going to be any other major groups or conventions in town that week?

12.   Sit in the lobby for a while and just observe. Are the guests greeted and taken care of as quickly as possible? Is the luggage taken care of quickly? Is there a line for the elevator or are there plenty of elevator banks to handle all the guests? This is another one of those "it happened to me" kind of stories. I booked a conference in Seattle, WA for 1100 people and there was always a long wait for the elevators! We got complaints left and right from everyone so I always make a point of seeing how many elevators the property has.

13. Is there plenty of parking for guests?

14. Is the property accessible for the handicapped?

I generally will present my client with a choice of three properties, with my first choice listed at the top. I will include all the brochures and prices from each property and present it to the client in proposal form. Now it is up to the client to choose. Once they do, you can begin negotiating the contract with the facility. Once negotiated, the client should sign the contract, not you. This way, if the meeting is canceled or something goes wrong, the hotel will hold your client responsible.

Contracts

Hotel contracts may look simple on the outside, but many have some clauses on the inside that could give you a major headache. If you cancel the event, find out from the salesperson exactly what you will be charged for. Some hotels will charge you for all the "lost revenue" that your group might have provided had the meeting not been canceled, and the wording is so vague in the contract that you might never find it. This means that the hotel can charge you for things like food, room service, room nights, and telephone calls. So, make sure the contract CLEARLY states what you will be charged for in case of cancellation. If a detailed description is not there, make them add it in before your client signs.

The contract should also clearly define the scope of the meeting, location of where the function is to be, date of the function and the function requirements. If there is only one room in the whole place that will suit your needs, MAKE SURE THEY WRITE IT IN! Otherwise, the facility has the right to put you wherever they deem appropriate. Of course, this is easier said than done, since many facilities will flat out refuse to do this. In this case, find out where they would move you to and then decide if you can live with it. If not, go somewhere else.

Also, try and get them to guarantee their food and beverage prices. If your event is months away, the chance that their food and beverage prices will go up is pretty high. So choose the menu BEFORE you sign the contract and get them to lock in their current prices.

Find out what group, if any, is going to be in there at the same time. What if you are having a wedding and the Oklahoma State Marching Band is having band practice right next door? Or, what if you are having a business meeting and there is a huge church revival with lots of singing taking place in the next room? These examples are obviously not likely to occur, but I am sure you get the point.

You can purchase our meeting/event planning contract that we use with our clients by simply going to our website. Again, be sure to have your own lawyer look it over before you use it.

To recap what we've done so far: we've discussed with our client what kind of party they want; established how much they wish to pay; and determined the date and general location for the event. Using these criteria we put together a list of possible sites for the function. We visited each site and presented our client with a list of the top three sites to choose from. The contract was negotiated and signed by the client. Now we are ready to move onto the next step ... logistics.

Logistics - Creating the Event

What exactly are logistics? Logistics are the nitty gritty details that go into planning an event. They include things like choosing the menu, typing up the name-tags, addressing the invitations, setting up the function room, calling the speakers to find out what their special needs are, and arranging for the audio visual equipment.

Let's take this one topic at a time.

Food and Beverage

The first thing you should do is find out if your client has a preference as to what to serve. If they do not, then offer suggestions based on their budget, guests and what the location has to offer. Put yourself in their shoes ... if you were one of the attendees, what would you want to eat?

As mentioned earlier, you also need to consider their budget. For example, if you are planning a wedding, then it might not be cost effective to hire the best caterer in town because of all the other costs involved. Remember the most expensive is not necessarily the best. If you are hiring a caterer then shop around. Ask your friends and neighbors who they have used in the past. Ask the caterer if you can sample their food. Ask for references and call them.

If you are working with a hotel, then the catering manager will be able to find you something suitable that is well within your budget. Remember that you don't necessarily have to stick to what they have on their menu. You can usually substitute things and work with the hotel's chef to design a meal that meets all your requirements and fits within your budget.

Here are some tricks of the trade that will keep your costs down:

1. For a breakfast, cut your breakfast pastries in half.

2. For a lunch, serve the dessert at your afternoon break. This is a great way to keep people awake during the afternoon because it gives them a little sugar boost and prevents you from having to buy something to go with the coffee and soda in the afternoon.

3. At a buffet, make sure the plates are small so the guests don't load up. Some people will make the reception their dinner and

will eat as much as possible so they can save money by not going to a restaurant.

4. Serve "dead stock wine" with the meal. Many hotels will routinely change their house wines from time to time and they might still have a few bottles of the "old" house wine left in their basement. So ask them about it! If they have some they will generally offer it to you at a discounted price.

5. If you must have a full bar at a reception then have a waiter standing at the entrance offering glasses of wine and silver platters of food to the guests as they walk in. Most people will not drink hard liquor once they have started with wine. The beauty of this is that it will create a very elegant atmosphere at your function. Waiters decked out in tuxedos and white gloves are a nice addition to any event.

6. Only pay for the bottles that have been opened. If you have a lot of half-full bottles left over at the end of the reception don't forget to take them home with you! You paid for them!

7. Have the bartenders measure each drink as opposed to free pouring.

8. Don't put the food on tables near the entrance. Instead put them at the back of the room so people have to search for them.

9. Have each food station manned by a waiter. Most people will not pile their plates high with food if someone is watching them.

10. If you are in a hotel, find out what other groups are serving and offer the same thing. The hotel will give you a discount because they will be able to buy in bulk.

11. Try to make sure that the coffee break is set outside of the room in the hall and not inside the room. The rattling of dishes and coffee cups can be very distracting.

12. Serve finger food at coffee breaks. There is nothing worse than trying to do a balancing act with your coffee cup and plate while trying to hold a conversation with someone. Keep it simple and elegant.

13. Don't forget about serving pasta and salad for lunch instead of the proverbial "rubber chicken." It is generally less expensive than other food items and people love it.

14. If your client wishes the function to have a theme of some kind, ask the hotel if they have any decorations in their basement that are leftover from previous groups.

15. Ask the hotel if you can "borrow" some of the plants from their lobby to use at your reception.

A really nice touch for out-of-town attendees at a meeting is to organize a dinner for them. Collect the menus from one or two local restaurants and mention to your clients that you will be calling them later in the day to make a group reservation. Then, place a sign up sheet near the registration area so that people can sign up to go to one of the restaurants for a "Dutch treat" dinner of networking and fun. Also, make sure the group's leader informs the group about the sign up sheet during the morning announcements.

At about 3:00 pm, close the sign-up sheets and call in the reservation. Everyone has a great time at these things. When traveling, I generally will not go out to a restaurant because I really hate to eat alone. I prefer to eat in my room if I have no one to go with. This solves this same problem for everyone. You can go out to a great restaurant and network with the other attendees while having a great time.

Try it!

Registration - Nametags

If you are planning a meeting of some kind, then chances are pretty good you will want each attendee to wear a nametag. You have two choices here:

1. You can have some blank "sticky" badges at a table by the entrance and the attendee can write their own badge.
2. You can offer each attendee a pre-printed computerized badge.

If you choose the latter, the company that we use is *pc/nametag*. To get a copy of their catalogue you can call them at 1-800-233-9767. They have some really excellent computer software systems for badges that are both versatile and reasonable. You can also find badge stock, plastic pin cases, ribbons and other items that will help make your meetings look professional.

Registration - Location and Staff

If you have to register people and hand out badges, then make sure that the registration table is easy to find. Don't put it in an out-of-the-way coatroom. Place it directly outside your main meeting room so that attendees can find it quickly and easily. Directional signs placed in the lobby are also helpful.

For a small group (up to 50) you will need at least one 8-foot table and a few chairs for the staff to sit on. However, if your client is handing out some materials you will need at least one additional table to place it on.

Expect to use an additional table for every 50 people. Larger groups should be divided alphabetically. If money is to be taken at the door, keep paid registrations separate from the unpaid. It helps to make the lines go quicker. It is also a good idea to have a separate "information" table so that people can ask questions without slowing down the line.

Also make sure that there are some comfortable seats for the attendees to sit on. Many like to get their registration materials and then go sit down and look at it. Complimentary beverages are also a nice touch if it is within the budget.

The local Convention and Visitors Bureau can also set up a table where people can get information on restaurants, tours, general information and maps of the area. This also adds a nice touch.

Your staff should be dressed in business attire and should be friendly and smiling. Remember that they will be representing your company and will be the first people that attendees see, so they must appear professional at all times. In fact, your local Convention and Visitors Bureau will be able to find you some registration personnel if you don't wish to tie up your own staff. These people are always well-trained and wonderful to work with!

Photographers, Florists, Decorations

Ask the client if they will be needing any photographers, videographers, press coverage, flower arrangements, speaker tables and/or registration tables.

A very nice thing to do is to place a sticker under ONE coffee cup at each table. The person who gets the sticker gets to take home the flower arrangement at their table. Another great thing to do at banquets and/or weddings is to place a disposable camera on each table. You can get some really wonderful candid pictures that the event's official photographer can't.

If your client has a theme or any special colors, ask the catering manager for your event if you have any choices for tablecloth color and decorations. You can also ask the catering manager what themes they have done in the past for other clients to get an idea of what might work for your group.

Don't forget about the invitations to the event! You can design a nice brochure or flyer that outlines the details of the function and gives information about where to send registration money, or, you can send out hand-written invitations. It really all depends on the type of function you are having.

Entertainment

Is there a special theme for the event? Perhaps a local trio of wandering musicians to greet the guests would be fun, or a magician wandering around doing tricks? Call your local CV&B for entertainment suggestions since they always have the inside track! (yes, I use them a lot, can you tell?) Local speaker bureaus can also give you some wonderful leads for entertainment. The catering manager for your event will also be a valuable resource for you because, remember, they've done this before hundreds of times! So don't be afraid to ask questions because that is what they're there for.

Before you finish making your plans, don't forget about security! If you have to store things overnight make sure the facility has a safe place for you to keep them. Are there going to be any VIP's that require additional security attending the meeting? Don't forget to ask your client! How about press coverage?

Planning a meeting or event doesn't have to be hard; it is just time consuming. When you think of something, write it down on a pad on your desk. Meeting planning is simply organizing the details for other people. Take things one at a time and keep yourself organized and you will do just fine. Write down exactly what you have to do and check off the items as you go because you will be less likely to forget something along the way.

Chapter 8

Business Proposals

Business proposals. Also known as RFP's (Request for Proposals). At some point in your business life you will eventually have to write one. In fact, most of us have to write dozens in order to get business. So how do you write an effective business proposal without giving away the store? Good question!!! When you figure it out just e-mail me! (*Just kidding*)

Each proposal should be customized to meet the client's particular needs. It should also be as short as possible while still covering all the major points.

There are seven parts to an effective business proposal.

Contact Information – Your proposal should have your contact information including name, company, address, phone, and e-mail. You could also give it a short title summarizing the entire proposal. Just don't make it long. It should be short, sweet, and to the point.

Overview – This is an overview of what you are going to do for them. It's not a detailed list, but more of a statement of the benefits you will provide them and a general overview of what you'll be doing for them. It could also include the history of your company or even the history of the concierge industry itself.

Dates/Times – When is the work going to start? How long is it going to take? If you are pitching an in-house/lobby concierge service, what will the hours be? How long is the contract for – one year, two?

Details - You should include some of the services that you specialize in, as well as an outline of your rates.

Ending Statement - I suggest that you end your proposal with a statement of exactly what you will produce for the client. Perhaps you'll want to talk about your customer service policy, or your business ethic. Answer the client's question - "What will I get if I hire this company, what makes them different from all the rest."

Extras – Although this one is optional, I always include it. Add client testimonials and press releases at the end of the proposal. You can also include a short biography of yourself and your company if you haven't already talked about this.

Always ask for the business!

Now I would like to give you a short word of warning. Years ago when Ron and I owned a meeting planning company we would often send out detailed proposals (that would take me days to do) and would never hear back from them. I remember one man in particular. This guy wanted us to plan an incentive meeting for his sales staff and asked for three different types of resorts and a professional facilitator to lead the weekend. It took me days, but I finally came up with three wonderful properties – one on the beach, one ranch in the west and one near a large city. I sent him a detailed proposal with our prices and a list of everything I could do and would do for him. Man … it was beautiful!!! The perfect proposal … or so I thought.

A few days went by and I followed up with a telephone call. Nothing.

I gave it another week and called again. Nothing.

He wouldn't return my calls or e-mails and we never heard from them again.

What happened?

Simple. He gave our detailed proposal to his secretary and had her implement it. The beautiful proposal that took me days to research and write ... they simply took as a map of sorts and did it themselves.

So my advice is to be careful. Don't give away the store like we did!!! Tell them what you can do for them ... not how you will do it. That was our mistake. Make your proposal just detailed enough so that they will completely understand what you will do for them. You want them to have confidence that this is a job that they couldn't possibly do themselves!!

Remember ... ALWAYS ask for the business! I suggest that you shake their hand firmly, look them directly in the eye and say - "We really want your business. What can we do to make this happen today?"

Lastly, if you go to the free article section on our website, you can find an article in there with over five pages of work/life statistics. People just love numbers, so please pick as many as you like from this article and add it to your business proposal, website and other marketing material. Here is the direct link: www.triangleconcierge. com/statistics.htm.

To read more about business proposals, you can pick up the book *The Consultant's Guide to Proposal Writing: How to Satisfy Your Clients and Double Your Income* by Herman Holtz. (More book suggestions are at the back of this book.)

I went into a McDonald's yesterday and said, 'I'd like some fries.' The girl at the counter said, 'Would you like some fries with that?'

Jay Leno

Chapter 9

Logistics
(What to do when the call comes in)

Mrs. Smith is on the telephone and would like you to book her vacation, find a hotel room, buy and stock her refrigerator with groceries and walk the dog while she's away. Great! Now how are you going to fill this request? What are the exact steps you are going to follow? In what order?

These questions all need to be answered, in full, so that you can provide Mrs. Smith with the best service possible. By writing a logistic script, not only will you know exactly how to fill this order, but your employees will know it too. Training new employees and temporary employees will be a snap because all they need to do is learn the steps from the script! Even if you are a one-man show right now and have no employees, the scripts will still be beneficial to you because you will logistically know how you are going to fill each request. In essence, it will flush out all the bugs from your system before you open up your doors!

Here are some sample scripts that I wrote a few years ago. They are very detailed and include many things (like an Ops Manager) that you might not need right now so take them with a grain of salt, so to speak. Please remember that they are simply samples and are only included to show you how detailed your own scripts can be. Your own script can be as detailed or as simple as you wish.

Sample Scripts

Errand Script

1. Telephone call comes in.
2. The errand form is completely filled out and the client information taken. What is needed, where, when and how the client will you pay.
3. Client is looked up in the database and their status is checked. Also checked is the status of their concierge account.
4. The call ends.
5. A copy is made of the form. Original (yellow) given to administrative/accounting and the copy (white) is given to operations (ops).
6. If order is to be done on the same day it is immediately taken to ops and handed to the manager.
7. If order is to be done on the next business day, then order is to be put in the ops box.
8. Administrative/accounting enters information into the computer and files the form in the pending file.
9. Ops receives the order and logs it onto their dispatch sheet.
10. They then assign the job to a driver and log the information onto the driver's trip sheet. Errand order form is also given to driver and attached to form.
11. If the errand is needed on the same day, ops will call the driver on their cell phone. Driver then will pull over to the side of the road and will add the pertinent information to their trip sheet.
12. Ops will put the driver's trip sheet and errand forms into a manila envelope, which the drivers pick up when they begin their shift. The driver also picks up enough cash to cover all the errands from accounting. Driver signs out money from accounting.
13. Driver does the errands.

14. Driver returns and gives his/her envelope to ops. Any leftover money is given to accounting.
15. Night ops manager will cross reference all the daily orders to make sure all the orders that had to be done were done. Receipts are matched with expenditures.
16. A copy of the driver log is made and put into the driver's file. The original driver's log, errand order form, receipts are all signed off and then given to accounting.
17. Accounting logs information into the compute, updates the concierge account, and generates any necessary invoices to either client or service vendors used.
18. White and yellow errand order sheet, driver log and other forms are all stapled together and the date and name of individual who completed the job(s) are written on the top. Forms are then filed under the client's name.
19. In-house errands/jobs such as meeting/event planning, word processing, information search and the like are entered onto the office board.

Signing up New Member Script

1. Telephone call comes in.
2. A new member application is filled out.
3. Pre-payment information is taken.
4. If errands needed, go to errand script.
5. If no errands needed then call ends.
6. Application information is entered into computer database.
7. Application is filed under new member's name.
8. Send new member a confirmation packet.

Business Referral Script

1. Telephone call comes in.
2. Client is looked up in database to find out if customer is active or not.
3. Client requests a business referral.
4. Staff member puts client on hold and goes and gets the Rolodex.
5. Staff member looks up the business referral in the Rolodex and gives information to the client. If client wants more choices, then go to number 9.
6. Call ends.
7. Staff member then calls the business that was referred and gives them the client name and telephone number.
8. Call ends.
9. If client wants more choices then client's telephone number is taken and client is told that it will be researched and someone will get back to them within the hour.
10. Staff member ends the call and logs onto Citysearch in the computer.
11. Staff member researches the information using the computer and the Yellow Pages.
12. Staff member then calls the client back with the appropriate information.
13. The call ends.
14. Information is logged into client's file in the computer.
15. Accounting is notified that a referral has been given.
16. In three days, the staff member who took the call makes a follow-up call to the client to find out how the referral was and if they were treated appropriately, etc…
17. At the end of the month, a statement is sent to each vendor that outlines the referral number, and the name of customer Vendor is to fill in the amount of job and the commission "blanks".

Vendor sends back the appropriate amount to Triangle Concierge.

Restaurant Reservation/Recommendation Script

1. Telephone call comes in.
2. Client is looked up in database to find out if customer is active or not.
3. Client requests a restaurant recommendation for the following night.
4. Staff member puts client on hold and goes into our restaurant database.
5. Staff member asks client what type of restaurant/food they would like and what city/location they wish to go.
6. Client answers.
7. Staff member looks up the appropriate restaurant and gives information to the client. If client wants more choices then client's telephone number is taken and client is told that it will be researched and someone will get back to them within the hour.
8. Staff member ends the call.
9. Staff member researches the information.
10. Staff member then calls the client back with the appropriate information.
11. Staff asks client if they would like us to make a reservation for them
12. If no, restaurant telephone number and information is given to client and the call ends.
13. If yes, what day and time would they like?
14. Information taken, and the call ends.
15. Staff member immediately calls the restaurant and makes the reservation for client.
16. Information is logged into client's file in the computer.

Dry Cleaning Script

1. Telephone call comes in.
2. Client is looked up in database to find out if customer is active or not. Concierge account status is looked up: how are charges to be processed - cash customer or credit customer?
3. Errand order form is completed.
4. Call ends by confirming order to customer. Order is assigned an order number and the number is given to customer.
5. Call ends.
6. A copy is made of the form. Original (yellow) given to administrative/accounting and the copy (white) is given to operations (ops) for routing.
7. Administrative/accounting enters information into the computer and files the form in the pending file.
8. Accounting puts a hold onto the customer's concierge account and then puts the form into pending file for completion.
9. Ops receives the order and logs it onto their dispatch sheet.
10. They then assign the job to a driver and log the information onto the driver's dry cleaning trip sheet. The Errand order form is also given to driver and attached to form.
11. If the errand is needed on the same day, ops will call the driver on their cell phone. Driver then will pull over to the side of the road and will add the pertinent information to his/her trip sheet.
12. Ops will put the driver's trip sheet and errand forms into a manila envelope that the drivers all pick up when they begin their shift. Driver also picks up enough cash to cover all the errands from accounting.
13. Driver does the errand by going to client's home and picking up their dry cleaning. Then driver goes to nearest Medlin Davis and drops off the cleaning under the client's name. The date the cleaning is to be ready is noted on the driver's Dry Cleaning Sheet.

14. Driver goes onto the next errand, or goes back to OPS and gives their envelope to OPS. Any leftover money is given to accounting.
15. Night OPS manager will cross reference all the daily orders to make sure all the orders that had to be done were done. Receipts are matched with expenditures.
16. Night OPS manager will note what day the cleaning is to be ready and logs it onto the appropriate daily dispatch sheet.
17. A copy of the driver's log is made and put into the driver's file. The original driver's log, errand order form, receipts are all signed off and then given to accounting.
18. On the appropriate day the cleaning is to be ready, OPS assigns a driver to go pick up the cleaning.
19. Driver picks up cleaning, logs the pertinent information onto their form and delivers cleaning to client's home.
20. Driver moves onto another errand. Once driver drops off his/her logs, Accounting logs information into the computer, updates concierge account, and generates any necessary invoices to either client or service vendors used.
21. White and yellow errand order sheet, driver log and other forms are all stapled together and the date and name of individual who completed the job(s) are written on the top. Forms are then filed under the client's name.

Modified House Sitting Script

1. Telephone call comes in.
2. Client is looked up in database to find out if customer is active or not. Concierge account status is looked up: how are charges to be processed - cash customer or credit customer?
3. Errand order form completed.
4. Call ends by confirming order to customer. Order is assigned

an order number and the number is given to customer.

5. Call ends.
6. A copy is made of the form. Original (yellow) given to administrative/accounting and the copy (white) is given to operations (OPS) for routing.
7. Administrative/accounting enters information into the computer and files the form in the pending file.
8. Accounting puts a hold onto the customer's concierge account and then puts form into pending file for completion.
9. OPS receives the order and logs it onto the appropriate daily dispatch sheet.
10. On the appropriate day, OPS assigns the job to a driver and log the information onto the driver's trip sheet. The Errand order form is also given to driver and attached to form.
11. If the errand is needed on the same day, OPS will call the driver on his/her cellphone. Driver then will pull over to the side of the road and will add the pertinent information to their trip sheet.
12. OPS will put the driver's trip sheet and errand forms into a manila envelope that the driver picks up when they begin their shift. Driver also picks up enough cash to cover all the errands from accounting.
13. Driver does the errand by going to client's home and picking up their mail and checking around the house.
14. Driver goes onto the next errand or goes back to OPS and gives their envelope to ops. Any leftover money is given to accounting. Client's mail is given to OPS.
15. Night OPS manager will cross reference all the daily orders to make sure all the orders that had to be done were done. Receipts are matched with expenditures.
16. Night OPS manager will note if another visit to the home is necessary and logs it onto the appropriate daily dispatch sheet if necessary.
17. A copy of the driver's log is made and put into the driver's file.

The original driver's log, errand order form, receipts are all signed off and then given to accounting.

18. On the appropriate day, driver visits the home again.
19. Number 13 and 14 are repeated.
20. Driver moves onto another errand.
21. Once driver drops off his/her log, Accounting logs information into the computer, updates concierge account, and generates any necessary invoices to either client or service vendors used.
22. White and yellow errand order sheet, driver log and other forms are all stapled together and the date and name of individual who completed the job(s) are written on the top. Forms are then filed under the client's name.

As a final note, remember that there are many concierge companies out there, and each one is unique. This is only one of the ways to set up your business. If you wish to see how the others are set up, just log onto the Internet and do a search on the word "concierge" and "errand." Read every single website, every page, and click on everything that you can possibly click on. You'll get the gist of how others are set up in no time.

Remember not to sell yourself short, you are a valuable person who is offering some new cutting edge services that will become invaluable to your community! If you undervalue your business, you are in effect undervaluing your services. Have faith in yourself and in the new services you are providing and you will do well. You are offering your clients one of the most valuable things in the world - **TIME**. More time to do the things that they want to. More time to spend with their family. More time to work at their desk. More time to actually eat lunch and not run errands. More time...the ultimate commodity.

Your concierge service is the wave of the future and its cutting edge services will alleviate a lot of stress, thereby creating a healthier environment for your client's family.

Finally, let me give you a little marketing tip. Whatever number
you come up with for your yearly membership (or retainer) fee …
divide that number by 52. For example, $250 divided by 52 would
equal $4.80 (these numbers are an example only). Your new sales
pitch can now be:

> "Where else can you get a personal assistant
> for only $4.80 per week?"

Many people have found this to be a great way to sell their
business!

Chapter 10

Service Vendors and Commissions

Service Vendors are an important part of your business because the commissions generated build an excellent revenue source without large expenditures. Therefore, profits grow! You want to pick the cream of the crop because, to be perfectly blunt, if your service vendors do a bad job you will be the one who will ultimately take the blame for it and you might lose the client because of it. There are several steps, however, that you can follow which should allow you to avoid this pitfall.

Commissions

There are two ways to set this up. You can charge the vendor a yearly fee or you can obtain a commission. Some companies are set up to obtain commissions of 10% from each vendor, other companies in larger cities obtain commissions of 15%.

Not everyone will actually give you a commission. Legally, realtors, lawyers and financial advisors are not allowed to, and travel agents only earn about 6% per ticket they book! (You can get a commission from large groups). As a service to your clients, I think that you should still refer people to service vendors who cannot give you a commission because you will receive generous referrals from them whenever you do. The reason is that they will be grateful and will tell others about your company and the wonderful service you provide. By the way, you can also barter with them by trading your referrals for various services they can provide. However, always try to get the commission first. You can tell them that they are gaining access to your numerous and valuable clients with no advertising costs. They would have to take out a print ad in a local paper, do a bulk mailing campaign, or even pay for an ad on their local radio station to get access to your clients. So your service is actually a huge savings for them!

Interviews and Contracts

It is important to not only interview service vendors that you sign on, but you should also have them sign a contract and fill out an application. Have them send you their business card and brochure for your files.

Some companies run their service vendors like a "leads group". In other words, they only put in <u>one</u> company per category (although a very complete and updated list of vendors is kept for all services). That way the service vendor is absolutely guaranteed the lead for their particular category. Interview each vendor and explain your business. Tell them what you expect from them … You expect first class service from each one of them and expect them to give you 100% each time you call. In exchange for this, they receive some fantastic leads and can often double their client base within months.

There are other companies who have several vendors per category. In this case, the interview process is the same because you still should receive first class service from each and every vendor you sign onto your service.

All of your service vendors should completely understand that if they do not give you quality service, do not return your calls in a timely manner, or if they do not treat your clients with the respect they deserve then you will replace them with their competitor in an instant. Customer service means everything in business today, and you should give 200% to every client and service vendor that you have.

Obtaining good service vendors, however, is a full time job in itself. Ultimately, you might want to consider hiring a service vendor representative, full or part time. This employee would find the service vendors, interview them and follow up with each one to obtain the commissions earned. It would be wise to have most of your service vendors on board <u>before</u> you open your new service up to your clients because once they start coming in your time will become even more valuable than it is now.

Where do I find the Service Vendors?

Ask all of your friends, family, acquaintances, and neighbors whom they have used personally. Personal referrals are always the best. If you have not already done so, you can also join your local Chamber of Commerce and send out letters to service vendors explaining what you are providing and asking them to sign on with you. I actually did a mailing like this and followed up with a telephone call and signed on some really great vendors. Once the nature of your service gets out, vendors will be calling you asking to be a part of your service. You can even ask vendors who you sign on for referrals to other vendors.

Don't go to the largest company in town because they have plenty of clients and really don't need you. In fact, most will not give you a commission because they are really not very hungry for your business. Instead, go to the little guys who are desperate for your business! Not only do they need clients (and will bust their hump to please you) but most will be willing to give you a commission! Now… logistics. The vendor fills out the contract and application form and sends you a brochure and business card. You can then put their business card into a Rolodex file (or a computer database) so you can give their name to a client at a moment's notice. I'm a bit old fashioned, so I use a two Rolodex files — one round for vendors and one square for personal/general office use so that you can distinguish between the two quickly. You can also create a database in your computer for your vendors so you can find them efficiently.

List of Service Vendors

The following is a list of service vendors. I listed as many as I could think of just to get you started.   This is by no means a complete list since every "service" business is a possible service vendor. The list is in alphabetical order.

- Accountant
- Air Conditioning/Heat
- Air Plane Charter
- Blinds and Curtains, Window Treatments
- Builder
- Carpet Cleaner
- Caterer
- Cleaning Professional
- Courier
- Decorator
- Dry Cleaner
- Electrician

- Errand Company
- Event Planner
- Financial Advisor
- "Fix-it" guy
- Florist
- Incentive Company (which sell promotional items like pens, mugs, shirts and the like)
- Insurance
- Landscaper
- Lawyer
- Maid service
- Meeting Planner
- Painter, Wallpaper Hanger
- Personal Chef
- Personnel Company
- Pet-Related Companies like veterinarians, pet-sitters and hidden fence companies
- Photographer
- Plumber
- Printer
- Realtor
- Sign maker
- Special Event Company
- Transportation Company (limousine, bus, town car, taxi service and the like)
- Trophy/Award/Plaque maker

How do I get the Commissions from the Vendors?

Logistically, there are thousands of ways to set this up. Most likely, you will have to negotiate with each vendor that you sign up to find out the method that works best for you. Here are some ways that others have set it up. Personally, I prefer the first, but I have seen companies have success with both methods.

1. (*My personal favorite*) ... You can take all the orders yourself. For example, you would advertise the same price that your vendor charges, arrange for the job, the client would pay you and you would pay the vendor. Then, when you actually do pay the vendor you would deduct the 10-15% commission from the bill's total.

2. You can charge your clients 10-15% more than the vendor's advertised prices.

Whichever one you use, please <u>make sure</u> that you get everything in writing detailing the fee structure as completely as possible.

At the end of this book, you'll find a sample vendor proposal for your convenience when creating your own letter. You will also find a sample vendor application so you don't have to re-create the wheel.

Chapter 11

Errand Service

There are two ways to set this up. First, you could outsource it to a local errand service company and obtain a commission on each run they make, or, you could do it yourself. If there is no errand company to outsource it to in your area, or you just want to do it yourself because of the additional revenue that you can make, here's how to set it up.

Finding the Drivers/Personal Shoppers

Placing an ad in your local paper's classified section will work. Another source for reliable staff can be found at local senior centers. Visit in person and ask if any seniors might want to run some errands to earn a little extra cash. They are reliable, honest and very hard workers! You can also use stay-at-home mothers who want to work part-time.

The drivers must be neat, presentable, and clean. You can require them to wear khaki pants or shorts and a collared shirt. Each driver can be given two magnetic signs for their car doors as well as business cards and brochures to hand out along the way. They are generally paid by the hour and full time drivers are eligible for benefits. Many companies provide their drivers with a company car to drive, which is a great idea once you have the financial base to pay for it. Drivers should also have a company ID clearly showing the client that they are your representative or employee.

Should I hire them as independent contractors or employees?

A very good question! Here is a brief answer ...

Independent contractors are not employees so you will not have to pay them the worker's compensation or benefits that you are required to pay an employee. You are also not liable for any negligent acts that they commit. If you hire a courier to take a box across town, for example, you are not liable for any damage or injuries that might happen during the course of the delivery of the box. If, on the other hand, the courier is an employee driving a company car, then you are responsible for anything that might happen. At the end of the year, you will be responsible for giving them the appropriate 1099 for their taxes (you should contact your accountant for the details on 1099's). The downside here is that you don't have any real control over "when" and "how" they are going to work.

Employees, on the other hand, can be required to wear certain clothes, have set work hours and a specific number of sick and vacation days. You can train them how to treat your clients and teach them the skills they need to perform their duties in order to maintain consistency within your company. You can teach and hire loyal, honest and reliable employees. With independent contractors you might not be able to establish any of these as they are not your employees. I am not saying that contractors won't be honest and reliable, I am merely pointing out that they won't be as loyal to you as an employee will.

If you need more information on this topic, then I suggest that you contact your lawyer or your certified public accountant.

Setting it up

In the beginning you will find yourself doing most of the errands. Hire each person one at a time, and slowly increase your staff as you increase your sales and revenue. Give each driver either a cell phone or a beeper so that you can contact them with changes or additions to their schedule.

Ideally, there should be one person in the office "dispatching" all the drivers, not to mention to get more business and make "sales" calls. In addition, try to coordinate drivers so that they may be able to run errands or shop for more than one customer at a time. For example, perhaps you have three clients and you have told the first client that her errands will take about 2 hours. The other two clients have been told that their errands will take one hour each. 4 hours on errands total. By combining the errands for these three people, the driver could potentially complete the errands in 3 hours, thereby saving time and increasing revenue.

Have the drivers keep ALL receipts and record EVERY errand they go on. Each driver should record exactly where they go and how much they spend on the daily trip sheet form (sample located in Chapter 18). They can either carry cash to pay for the errands or a company credit/debt card. If possible, set up credit with the businesses that your company uses most often.

It is probably easiest in the long run to set up your business so that you can accept credit cards. Then your customer can give you their credit card to keep on file and you can charge whatever errands you run for them to the card. If, however, you are not set up for credit cards you can create a concierge account for them before you run the errand. For example, Mrs. Smith wants you to pick up some groceries, go to the drug store and post office, buy some special food for the dog at the vet's and then run to the frame store to buy a few frames for some pictures she has. You should ask her to deposit $100 into her concierge account. Then, you use this money to run the errand and you can either bill her for the balance (if there is any), or she can pay you on the spot with a check when you deliver her supplies. You can also ask each client to keep a minimum balance in their account (like $200 for example) to use to pay for the errands.

If you plan on actually going into people's homes, then it will be helpful for you to keep a key-rack of some sort in your office since many clients prefer you to keep a copy of their key so they don't have to be bothered.

A very nice touch is to send each client a personal thank you note after they use your service. We have a carpet cleaner who sends us a handwritten thank you note after he cleans our carpets! This personalized touch keeps me from using anyone else and I have referred him to more people than I can count.

I also suggest that you have each employee sign a non-competition clause because the last thing you want to do is to train your competitors.

Accepting Credit Cards — E-commerce

We have done a great deal of research on this topic and have looked into a bunch of companies that will set you up to accept credit cards. It is an ideal way to do business because clients find it easier to just give you their credit card number to pay for services as opposed to giving you a check.

There are many different credit card services and banks who will help you set up your merchant account so that you can begin to accept credit cards. You can accept Visa, Mastercard, American Express, Discover Card and you can buy, lease equipment or do it via the web on a virtual terminal. We suggest that you do yourself a favor and do some research and comparison-shopping. Look around and see what the best deal is! Look up the word "merchant account" in the Yellow Pages, on the Internet or ask someone you know for a referral. Ask your bank as they might have a great program available.

You can also use PayPal at www.paypal.com if you don't want to set up a merchant account right away.

Do the research to find the best rates and fees, but please do not forget about service! The lowest fees for a service might not be the best one for your service as they might not be able to meet your specific needs.

One suggestion we can make is *Quickbooks* -- you can get a merchant account through them easily and quickly. I use Quickbooks myself and really like the software.

Real integrity is doing the right thing, knowing that
nobody's going to know whether you did it or not.

Oprah Winfrey

Chapter 12

Your Staff

In the beginning, you are the staff. Once you get your business up and running, however, you will have to hire people to help you. I suggest that you hire one person at a time according to your budget. As your gross sales increase, your staff can increase.

In a perfect world you might have the following (just to name a few):

1. Errand Drivers/Personal Shoppers
2. Bookkeeper and/or accountant
3. Service Vendor Coordinator to find and interview the vendor, sign the contract and follow-up.
4. In-house concierges filling the requests that come in via e-mail, phone and fax.
5. Sales/Marketing person
6. Lobby concierges as necessary
7. Operations Manager
8. Office Manager
9. Administrative Assistant

Remember that a happy employee will work harder and stay longer, so I suggest you try and be as "family friendly" as possible.

Work out a flexible schedule whether it is for a sick child or to attend a school performance. As long as they get their work done it should be no problem to accommodate your staff. If you need them to work with you until 9 pm at night, why not buy them a little dinner or order in a pizza? Treat your employees as you would treat your own family. Treat them like you would like to be treated if you were in their shoes. In fact, put yourself in their shoes and ask yourself "What would I want and how would I want to be treated?"

Putting honesty, integrity, and love first will only help increase your business. Nice guys DO finish first. If you are honest, ethical and trustworthy about everything that you do, not only will you receive repeat business from your clients, but you will also get 110% from your staff.

Of course I would not shoot myself in the foot either. Run both a state and federal background check on each of your employees. Go down to your local police department and ask them to run it for you. It is very inexpensive and well worth it. I would also run a credit check on each employee. Your employees need to be as honest as you are. If they see a $1000 bill on a client's kitchen table when they come in, it should be there when they leave.

The Hiring Process

Here are a few tips to help you minimize hiring mistakes. First you need to complete a profile of the perfect employee. Determine what skills and personal characteristics you wish them to have. Do NOT become desperate (even if you feel like you are) because it will only cause you to lower your standards and will lead you to believe that someone is qualified when they are not. Hiring incompetent people will just make everyone unhappy and will ultimately lead to problems.

Make up a list of "must have" and "would like to have." List those qualities that are related to skills, educational and work experience, behavior, and personality that you would like your ideal candidate to have. Use this list to ask open-ended questions in the interview. For example, "Can you describe to me the last time you handled an angry customer?"

Pay attention to the way they dress. Are they neat and clean? Were they on time for the interview? Are they sitting in the chair leaning forward or are they slumped back? When they talk about their past job which word do they use more frequently "I" or "we"? Using "we" indicates someone is a team player.

After the interview, if possible, have a co-worker or your business partner take the candidate to lunch. Their guard will be down and they will be more apt to behave naturally.

Once you hire the employee make sure they get off to a great start and be prepared for them. If they get off to a good start they will be motivated contributors from day one. Have their business cards ready and desk all set up. Everything they need should be ready by the time they arrive for their first day at work. Assign them a "buddy" to help them their first week. Ideally, this person would introduce them to your staff, give them a tour of the office, take them to lunch, fill them in on the company culture, and answer all their questions. Of course, if they are your first or second employee then you will be the buddy!

Finally, as boss you should meet with your new employee at the end of each day for the first week to make sure they are settling in and address any questions they might have. Letting a newly hired employee know how valuable they are from the beginning will only help you and is a really great company policy to have.

At the end of this book you'll find a few sample concierge job descriptions as well as some same interview questions to help you get started.

I have not failed.

I've just found 10,000 ways that don't work.

Thomas Edison

Chapter 13

Sales and Marketing

Now that you've set your business up you are ready to start work. Let the phone begin to ring! The following chapter is filled with some useful tips to help you get started with the sales and marketing.

Know Your Business

This may sound redundant, but it is also true. Know your business. Be able to "talk the talk." Know it inside, outside, backwards and upside down. You should, by now, be able to talk about every aspect of your business to anyone who asks. Energy and excitement should creep into your voice as you explain it to people. They should both feel and see your energy as you talk and "sell" to them. Show your excitement!

Now don't get me wrong, I am not suggesting that you leap around the room doing back-flips, I am merely suggesting that you don't hold back your excitement. Your excitement will infuse their excitement. Your positive energy will cause their positive energy. Talk to everyone you know about it - your neighbors, family, everyone. Network with everyone because everyone is a possible client. Get excited! It also helps to have some facts and figures to use in your conversation.

Feel free to use the figures I included in the introduction to this book, since it will demonstrate your knowledge of your business.

Professional Image

There are three things that you need as a sales professional. The first is the proper clothing, and I can't stress this enough because you want the client to remember your service NOT what you wore. This also does not necessarily mean a business suit. You should be clean and neat. Your style of clothing depends of what service you are providing. For example, if you were pitching a corporate client or real estate management company, then I would suggest suitable business attire. If, on the other hand, you are running errands on behalf of the company, then I suggest pants and a collared shirt of some kind, perhaps with your company logo on it. Anything you wear should be clean, neat and wrinkle-free.

You are the image of your company, so you should dress appropriately at all times. If you leave a lasting impression then both you and your company will be remembered. Make that first impression a lasting one because you may not get a second chance.

Speech

You also need to speak and write well. If you mumble, ramble on and don't have a clear command of the language, then you will not be taken seriously. You will have to have both one-on-one conversations, as well as group presentations. If you want corporate clients then most likely you will be asked to present your services to them at their next business meeting. Many community colleges and universities offer non-credit courses in public speaking. There are also some really wonderful books written on the subject.

The written word is also very important because it is our written word that people most often see first in brochures, sales letters, websites and in the sales kit. There are some nice software programs out there that will help you edit your letters and text as well as some really great books. Taking the time to be a better writer is worth it.

Remember, your investment into your company must include an investment into yourself so that your presentations, both oral and written, are strong!

Manners and Etiquette

There is more to this than just putting your napkin in your lap, not slurping your soup and not interrupting. You will be required to not only hold conversations with people, but will have to dine with them on occasion, meet them in their homes and make introductions. Being honest, sincere, friendly and polite is a major part of concierge work. Good manners may not help increase your clientele, but it will help prevent embarrassing moments that may lose them.

Take the time to learn the customs and culture of your international clients to make them feel more comfortable and to prevent any embarrassing slip-ups. For example, when you are given a business card from a Japanese client it is important to accept the card with both hands and bow in acceptance. Do NOT write anything on the card as they consider this extremely rude.

The Handshake

I know what you're thinking "Handshake? Now you've gone too far!" Well, hear me out first. The following article was written for exhibitors at a trade show, but actually applies to everyone even remotely associated with sales. The data suggests that just this small simple gesture can make a world of difference to your results.

Also, make sure that you don't sqeeze the hand too hard if you are a man, and for the ladies - no limp-fish handshakes please! Don't pump their arm like a water spout either. Lastly, make sure that you look directly into their eyes when you shake their hand because eye contact is just as important.

Put it There
By Dr. Allen Konopacki

In an age where the word communication conjures up images of phone lines and video screens, a trade show seems like the one place where meeting in person is still an important concept.

The success of the trade show industry proves that even in a world where technology reigns supreme, nothing is as effective as face-to-face contact.

Yet, a new study suggests that exhibitors are leaving out a key element for making in-person meetings valuable: the handshake. The study, conducted by the Incomm Center for Trade Show Research, found that in theory, practice and fact, a little shake of the hand goes a very long way towards giving your booth a boost.

Theory

Why do handshakes matter? They create warmth, trust and a sense of an immediate mutual relationship. They are also a great way to make your exhibit stand out from the others. **People tend to remember a person who greets them with a handshake more than those who don't**, and they'll be more likely to return to that person's booth because they felt welcome.

The first time you greet someone is critical because a relationship is usually established in the first four seconds of contact. There's an art to working trade shows successfully, and using a handshake can create a positive impression that can eventually win you sales.

Practice

To better understand the importance of handshakes, the following experiment was conducted for the study. A group of students left a quarter in a public phone booth. After strangers used the phone and took the coin, one of the students walked up to ask if they had seen the quarter. Of the roughly 75 people who were approached, over 40 lied, saying that they had never seen the 25 cents they had pocketed.

The experiment was then tried with another group of 75 strangers, with the difference being that the student greeted the person with a quick handshake and an introduction, then asked if the quarter had been spotted. Of this group, the number of people who fibbed dropped to 18 of the 75.

The conclusion was simple: handshakes create a higher degree of intimacy and trust within a matter of seconds. In fact, the gesture carries perhaps more weight than ever because so many face-to-face encounters have been replaced by phone calls, faxes and e-mail. A handshake is perceived as being reserved for personal attention.

Fact

Examples are all fine and good, but the evidence that handshakes have an actual effect is based on hard numbers. Here are the industry facts: Only 8 percent of exhibit sales representatives greet visitors at a trade show exhibit with a handshake. Even worse, the typical greetings used by salespeople, such as "Can I answer any questions?" or "May I help you?" are impersonal, and thus reduce comfort and trust.

When greeted with a handshake, 76 percent of individuals respond by being more open, friendly and honest. Salespeople who shake hands with a prospect or customer are twice as likely to be remembered compared to those salespeople who don't shake hands. In short, handshakes build a higher degree of interaction and memorability.

The previous article was reprinted with permission from Trade Show Ideas, a publication of the Trade Show Exhibitors Association, McCormick Place, 2301 South Lake Shore Drive, Suite 1005, Chicago, Illinois 60616, http://www.tsea.org

Sales Presentation

You might be asked to make a sales presentation to a corporate client. GREAT! Be prepared and know your client and you will do fine. Remember that you are selling an intangible service. A service that many people have never heard of or even considered. It is your job to bring this service to life through your presentation and enthusiasm.

The following tips can be used for both one-on-one presentations and group:

1. Make sure each attendee at the meeting has something to hold in their hands like a sales kit or your brochure.

2. Customize the materials inside the kit as much as possible by putting the client's name on it in several places. Make sure the information is updated and fresh.

3. Directly relate your service to the client's business. How your service will directly affect their employees, and what your service will do to make their job easier. Also explain how your service works.

4. Research the company for facts and figures to add to your presentation. It always pays to do your homework. If you are pitching a real estate management company, visit their properties and see which ones can have a lobby concierge.

5. Get the client involved. Ask them to turn to another page. Get them to ask questions.

6. Know the result you want...plan for the outcome. What do you want the presentation to accomplish? Do you want to just introduce your service or do you want them to actually sign a contract with you?

7. If appropriate, create a short PowerPoint presentation so they have something to look at while you speak.

8. Create a list of possible objections the client might have and prepare an answer for each one.

9. Ask the client if there is any reason this service might not work for them. It is better to get everything onto the table all at once so you can address each issue rather than leave with them hanging in

the air. Try the "feel, felt, found" method — I know how you feel, I felt the same way, but what I have found is this… This method allows them to not feel bullied into accepting something they're not sure they want.

10. Be friendly. Smile. Maintain eye contact and listen to their replies. Lean forward instead of leaning back and relaxing. Look excited! Take notes. Think before you speak!

11. When closing you can either give them a few alternatives or be completely honest and direct and ask for the business outright. Ask for the business, the worst thing that they can tell you is no.

12. Listen! The best sales people are the best listeners. If you don't listen, you may miss the point where they are ready to buy your product or service.

13. Follow up with the client and be reachable through e-mail, fax and cellphone. Make sure to thank them for their time!!

14. Make sure that you return ALL telephone calls and e-mails within twenty-four hours. Don't burn your bridges with this one. If it's a sales call that you really don't want to return, just remember that you never know who they might know and can refer your company to. What if they happen to be the daughter of IBM's president? You just never know. So do what I do, return everyone's call within twenty-four hours or less no matter who they are.

15. Finally, show them your dependability by following through with any request that they might make.

Sales Techniques and Tips

Since one of your major roles will be selling services to customers, I thought I would provide you with a few tips and techniques to make it easier.

First, please remember that today's customers are smarter and better informed than they were in the past. Why? Because they don't want to be "sold" something. They want the sales process to be easy, pleasant and productive. They want over-the-top customer service, which, of course, is the hallmark of the concierge industry. The key here is to let the potential client know about your company and its services without the hard sell.

68% of customers don't follow through on the sale because of a perceived attitude or indifference toward them by the owner, manager, or an employee of the company! *(Source: Customer Service Institute, Silver Spring, MD)*.

This shows that a positive experience between a customer and an employee has a greater impact on customer loyalty than advertising does.

Imagine, all the money you spent last year on marketing and it was simple customer service that brought you the customers.

I'll say it again - people determine customer loyalty. It's the number one way Ron and I have grown our business ... extreme over-the-top customer service. Make sure your customers' experiences with you are excellent before AND after the sale, and offer as much personal attention as you can.

Here are a few tips ...

ALWAYS be courteous to them 100% of the time! Smile and be pleasant no matter what.

Treat the customer with respect, each and every time.

The customer is always right, even when they're wrong, the customer is always right. SERVICE is your number one priority!

NEVER ignore a customer. If you see they've been waiting longer than two to three minutes, then walk over to them! If you are busy with another customer, politely excuse yourself and tell the waiting customer that you know they are there and that you will be with them in one minute.

Give the customer what they want, and not what you think they want. Don't talk ... LISTEN! This way you'll know exactly what their needs are.

We find that it's always a good idea to try and relate your service to the client's business and/or lifestyle. Always ask them probing questions (without getting personal) to find out what they do and what type of problems they are having. How will your service make their job and/or life easier? Also explain how your service works.

Know the result you want and then plan for the outcome. What do you want to accomplish? Do you want to just introduce your service or do you want them to actually sign on with you? It might help to prepare a list of possible objections the client might have and prepare an answer for each one.

You can also ask the client if there is any reason this service might not work for them. It is better to get everything onto the table all at once so you can address each issue rather than leave with them hanging in the air.

Laslty, when closing, you can either give them a few alternatives or be completely honest and simply ask for the business outright. You might say "We really want your business, so please let me know if htere is anything that I can do to help you." Make sure to thank them for their time!

Relationship Marketing

One of the first things that you have to understand about marketing is that it is completely different from sales. A salesman is trying to sell you something, a marketer is trying to develop a relationship with you.

A good marketer instinctively knows that he'll develop more customer loyalty if they are a friend. Wouldn't you rather do business with a friend?

For example … Matthew needs his house painted. After finding two reputable companies he calls them both up requesting bids. Company A comes out and is all business … he walks around the house asking only a few questions and leaves quickly promising to send the bid sometime next week.

Company B comes out and as he's walking around the house he begins to chat with Matthew asking him about what he does for a living and the like. Before long the two are chatting about sports as they wander around the house. When he leaves, Company B shakes Matthew's hand, gives him a brochure and business card, and promises to send the bid by the next day.

When the bids arrive, Matthew discovers that both companies are going to cost the same amount. Now who do you think Matthew gives the work to? Plus, when Matthew's friend Jeremy needs his house painted, who do you think he referred?

Relationship marketing is all about developing friendships. Longterm friendships that provide you with customer loyalty and referrals.

Always think about building a relationship and try and use these "relationship selling" techniques to make the sales process friendlier.

Here are a few more reasons why relationship marketing works ...

1. Relationship marketing may help get you business later if the buyer is not ready to purchase now.

2. Relationship marketing will give the potential client a strong feeling of trust, which will cause them to talk to others about you and refer you out.

3. It will build your external sales force. Your clients who will love you so much that they'll sell your company and its services to their friends and associates.

4. With a relationship comes a sense of obligation. The client will not be willing to move onto someone else as quickly because they already have a good relationship with you.

Your Marketing Plan

There are dozens of books out there on this topic, so the following is just a little something to get you started.

If you wish to create a formal marketing plan, then there are a bunch of books and software out there that will help you. In fact,

Entrepreneur Magazine has a host of articles on this subject that can be found at www.entrepreneur.com. However, unless you are getting funding from a bank or investor, you don't really need a "formal" plan.

If this is the case, what you need (in my humble opinion) is a simple marketing plan. A simple roadmap that will clearly show you where you are now, where you plan to go and what roads you will take to get there.

The Six-Step Marketing Plan

1. Company and Products Analysis -- What is your product? What services are you providing?

2. Target Audience - Who are you going to offer these services to? List the people or the different types of businesses that you want to go after. Describe your future clients in terms of population, demographics, income levels , etc.

3. Strategies - How are you going to get to these people. How are you going to get their attention? Brainstorm! Write down as many things as possible no matter what they are. Don't erase anything, just brainstorm all the ways you might get your business/services to these people.

4. Objective/Goals - What is your objective? Where do you want to be this time next year?

5. Budget - Lastly, you need to figure out your marketing budget.

Although many marketing ideas are free, some carry a cost such as placing advertisements in newspapers and magazines, creating brochures, flyers and the like. Having a budget will help control your spending.

6. Follow-up – after you've written your marketing plan, I suggest that you put a note on your calendar to read it again and re-visit everything six months from now. How are you doing? What worked and what didn't? What should you do differently? What products worked and what didn't? Is your pricing working or should you modify it? Then make the changes and try again! Persistence and determination is the key.

35 Ways to Market Your Business

For beginners, the first step in growing your new business is to find the customers. For those of you who are already up and running, the next step (now that you have clients) is that you must continue to generate new business every month, even if you have dozens of clients and no time for marketing! Why? Because there might come a day when the clients are not there, and it quickly becomes a very lean month when the phone doesn't ring. This is not the time to begin marketing ... the time to market is now.

Here are some cost-effective tips on where to find clients. Please note that not every tip will work for everyone. It really depends on both the type of service you have and who you are marketing to. Persistence is the key here! Don't give up after only one or two tries because it might take more. If fact, a potential client might have to read or hear about you anywhere from 5 to 18 times before they make a decision to buy.

Remember that you are selling an intangible service that everyone needs, but none of them think that they need it. So it is up to you to convince them of its value, and this generally takes time.

E-mail signature

Most e-mail software programs allow you to put an automatic signature at the bottom of your e-mails. You know ... those few lines of contact information at the bottom of an e-mail. People love it when you make information easy to find. In fact, e-mail is such a part of our lives now, that most people are more likely to grab your phone number off your latest e-mail than to dig up your business card. So what should go on your sig file? Your name, title, company name and your company tagline. You should also include your address, phone, cell phone, fax number, e-mail address and your Website address. Now, also consider putting promotional info in your sig file, such as an offer for a free report or product, a free consultation or trial offer, company announcement (new client, new product, award won, etc.), a hyperlink to your latest press release, article, or Web site feature or an invitation to subscribe to your free e-newsletter.

Include a return envelope

If you'd really like a response from a personal letter, include a return envelope in it with a live stamp on it. It'll increase your response or it'll drive them nuts.

Post advertising circulars on all the free bulletin boards

Post circulars in your area, especially the coin-operated laundries, grocery stores, and beauty and barber shops.

Always acknowledge

Always acknowledge when something nice is done for you with a thank you letter. No, a call is not the same.

Write articles for magazines and newspapers

Each time your articles are published, you gain credibility and visibility.

Develop a "small town" marketing approach

Send out congratulatory notes for weddings, graduations, and birthdays.

Stand-by space

Many publications will give you a contract for "stand-by" space. In this arrangement you send them your ad, and they hold it until they have unsold space, and then at a price that's always one third or less than the regular price for the space you need, insert your ad. Along these lines, be sure to check in with the suburban and neighborhood newspapers.

Headlines

Use headlines on your website, brochure and sales kit. Talk about how customers will benefit from your services, do not simply list what services your business offers. An excellent way to get attention is to boldly give the 5 or 6 key benefits of your product or service. Put the biggest benefit on top and list off the rest in descending order of importance. The best formula for creating headlines in marketing is "New product offers benefit, benefit, benefit." Use this to create the headline of your press releases and advertisements, for envelope teaser copy, and for the beginning lead of your brochure. For example:

How Would You Like To Get: Biggest benefit, Second biggest, Third biggest benefit ... You get the idea.

Become a guest on as many of the radio and television talk shows

Become a guest on as many of the radio and television talk shows or interview type programs as possible. Actually, this is much easier to bring about than most people realize. Write a letter to the producer of these programs, then follow up with an in-person visit or telephone call. Your initial contact should emphasize that your product or service would be of interest to the listeners or viewers of the program, perhaps even saving them time or money.

Provide GREAT customer service

This is the key to your success. If you tell people that you are going to give them more time, then you must take it one step further and value their time. Return ALL telephone calls and emails in 24 hours or less. This one thing has done more to grow Triangle Concierge than anything else we've done. Our reputation for fantastic customer service has given us more referrals than anything else.

Proof

Nobody wants to be a fool, or get robbed. Before buying anything, everyone wants to know if the money they're paying is worth the product or not. In this case, the proof is in the testimonials from your clients. Nothing works better than word of mouth because people want to know how the other person has benefited from your product.

Join your local Chamber of Commerce and go to all their networking functions

The key here is to network, network, network! Talk to everyone that you can about your new business. Hand out your business cards to everyone you meet! I like the cards that are folded where your information appears on the top and a quick list of your services is inside - a sort of mini-brochure.

Purchase the Chamber's mailing list and send out your brochure, business card and a short letter to each member

The cost will range in price from $20 to $200 depending upon where you live. Follow each letter up with a telephone call. You can also use your local Yellow Pages or any mailing list from your marketing area.

Develop a mailing list and send them a mailing every month

Develop a newsletter and send it out every other month. Send out special gift certificates or two-for-one dinner special coupons from a local restaurant. You need to stay in front of someone at least 5-18 times before they will respond to you so persistence is the key with marketing. Get the names from business cards you have obtained, membership lists from organizations that you belong to, your rolodex file, etc. Remember to keep it updated!

Create a website

Triangle Concierge gets 99% of its clients from our website and from referrals. Your website will enable thousands of people to find about you and your new service quickly and easily. Remember, however, that once created you MUST submit your site to search engines at least once a month. If they cannot find you when doing a search, then your website is not working for you.

Send out a press release to all the newspapers, television and radio stations in your area announcing your new business

This is one of the best ways to grow your business -- and it doesn't cost you a cent to do!

Advertising

Place an ad in your local newspapers, yellow pages, magazines or business journals, although this can be expensive. Also see if you can get an article written about your company. Ask!! Send them your press release!

Network, network, network!!

Go to every networking function you can find. Attend all the local expositions and hand your business card out to everyone you can. Network, network, and network!

Trade Shows

You can either be one of the exhibitors at a local exposition, or you may simple attend one and hand out business cards to everyone you meet. Both are valuable. It is also a nice way to obtain service vendors for a business referral service. Print a number of business cards to hand out. Don't forget to use both sides of the card with the company information on one side and a list of services and benefits on the other.

Ask the owner of a local coffee shop if you can put some brochures on his/her counter

I have many clients who have told me that this is one of the best ways they have found to grow their business.

Collect business cards. Make contact with anyone in the corporate environment

Place signs on every errand running vehicle

Read the business section of your local newspaper and look for company and personal leads

Ask!

Ask friends, neighbors and family for leads and contacts.

Visit your local spas

Propose that they include errand running with their all-day packages. As the clients get pampered, you run their errands for them! By the end of the day not only do they feel great, but their errands are all done. This idea would also work for hair and nail salons.

Contact local surgeons

Often they will send home a patient with orders for complete and total bed rest. And, if that patient's spouse can't boil water, then its trouble! Offer 1 or 2 hour errand gift certificates that the surgeon can give to his/her patients who are recovering from surgery. Also, the surgeons themselves (as well as the nurses) are notoriously busy people and might benefit from your new service.

Go to your local country club or golf course

Offer to make your services a part of one of their membership packages. Logistics are great because 9 times out of 10 the member lives within a 5-mile radius of the club. Another good idea is to offer a golf package ... tee off and gives us your "to do" list. When you reach the 18th hole your errands are done and in the trunk of your car ready to go!

Affiliate with a local professional organizer company

Many professional organizers will have a client that not only needs help with organizing their lives, but with their daily tasks as well.

Get to know some local realtors ... notoriously busy people!

How about the airport?

Pilots and airline attendants are away for days at a time and might need a little helping hand once in a while.

Contact travel agencies

Ask them about offering pet-sitting or house-sitting services to their out-of-town clients.

Previous colleagues and associates

Remember the people you used to work with in your last job? Remember how you liked each other? Well, somehow over the years you have lost track of them. Now is the time to re-kindle those lost friendships. Watch where they lead ... you might be surprised! Add them to your mailing list to keep in touch with them. Your new newsletter is a great way to keep in touch with them.

Run special promotions and incentives

Make a contribution to a local charity's fundraiser by offering some free errand hours as a door prize. Perhaps contact your local "welcome wagon" and add a gift certificate to their package. A tip: always attach a list of services to the gift certificate so that they know what they can use it for.

Volunteer

Volunteer at events in your town ... you never know who you will be standing next to!

Have no doubts!

Want to know the secret of growing your business? The REAL secret? Change your words. I'm serious, change your words and you will change your life. Don't listen to the negative people who are telling you that your business will fail in today's economy. Turn your back on people who tell you that perhaps you should consider a 9 to 5 job. KNOW that you can do this! Have no doubts about it and turn your thoughts to "I am going to succeed!" and "I can do this."

The Ten P's of Success

1. **Plan** – Create a business and marketing plan

2. **Publicity** – print or electronic media, radio, television, direct marketing, networking.

3. **Persistence** – Don't give up!!

4. **Passion** in what you're doing.

5. **Product** - know your product inside and out!

6. **People** - understand the people you are selling to! They're not just clients ... they're real people and you can talk to them. No matter who you talk to, remember that they are a person first. Everyone on the planet puts their pants on one leg at a time.

7. **Prioritize** – don't do too much at once. Pick 5-10 things and then do them. Don't be so widespread - know what you're going to do first.

8. **Places** - Network, network, network! Go to every networking function that you can find. Build an army of people who heard about you through word-of-mouth.

9. **Promote** - Market for new clients even when you don't need any. Sure this month you have more work than you can handle, but what happens if the client pool runs dry next month. Then what? NEVER stop marketing!!!

10. **Plus**! Always give them more than they expect ... go the extra mile. Customer service should be your number one priority!!!

Lastly, don't let people tell you no! When they tell you "no" ask "why not?" Ask them why they are saying no ... is the price too high? Do they already use a company for this service? ASK THEM! The more information you have about why they are sayting "no" to you, the quicker you can make an adjustment to get them to say YES!

The only thing to do with good advice is pass it on. It is never any use to oneself.

Oscar Wilde

Chapter 14

Customer Service Can Make or Break your Business

Here's a nasty little fact I picked up a few years back … over half of your customers who stop using your services usually do so because of employee rudeness and bad customer service. The moral here is that over-the-top customer service makes all the difference and can literally make or break your business.

Over the years, we've run into some VERY bad customer service and it's really irritating!! Why don't people get it? It really goes without saying that if you're rude to me on the telephone or in person, I certainly am not going to want to use your product (or service) again, and I might even tell a few people about it! If you are nice to me, however, and go out of your way to help, then I'm going to recommend you to everyone I know.

I can't stress enough how important good customer service is to your business. No matter what business you are in. Customer service should be your number one priority!!! Not only is it extremely professional, but it shows the client that you respect them. The way you treat a client at first contact is critical because if they have a bad first experience, they'll never use your service. As they say, you don't get a second chance to make a good first impression.

Now I completely understand that it is normally not the principle/

owner who answers the phone, but that is no excuse! If your staff is rude and answers the phone (or greets the customers in person) with a bad attitude then how do you think it will reflect on you and your business? Be sure your staff provides the best in service, is courteous, respectful and honest to everyone and your business is sure to shine.

How did Ron and I grow our own business? By answering each and every telephone call and e-mail within 24 hours or less - more often than not, the same day. We treat all our clients like family and always put their needs first, no matter what.

One last tip … never ever put down a competitor when you are pitching your service or product to a client as it's bad business and shows a complete lack of respect. If a company pitches their service or product to us in this manner, we won't do business with them. Don't get us wrong, competition is good!!! It's fine to want to win a contract with a prospective client, just do it in an honest and ethical manner. I'll be talking about competition a bit more further into this chapter.

Treat everyone (including your competitors) with respect, kindness, honesty and love … basic spiritual principles that everyone should apply to their business.

A few Customer Service Tips ...

Superior customer service improves everyone's morale, productivity and employee retention.

1. ALWAYS and I mean ALWAYS return telephone calls and emails within 1-2 business days (sooner if possible). Even if you don't have an answer for them, just give them a courtesy call that you aware of it. How can you tell people that you want to give them more time if

you don't respect their time? Treating others like you would like to be treated will only cause positive things to happen ... and your reputation for providing great customer service and caring about your employees will spread like the proverbial brushfire.

2. Say "thank you." I mean this ... a simple genuine "thank you" goes a very long way with people.

3. Exceed their expectations. When someone goes above and beyond the call of duty how do you feel? Happy? Most people feel positive about the experience, and they will tell everyone they know about it!

4. Your organization must make good customer service your number one priority.

5. Solicit feedback. What do people want from your company? Ask them! Then talk to them afterwards to find out how it went. Make it easy for people to give you feedback ... ask them personally via telephone or e-mail.

"The goal as a company is to have customer service that is not just the best, but legendary."
Sam Walton

"To give real service you must add something which cannot be bought or measured with money, and that is sincerity and integrity."
Donald A. Adams

The customer's basic needs

Your clients have a few basic needs. They want friendliness, courtesy and respect. They want to know that you appreciate their needs and circumstances and they want your attention and reasonable answers to their questions. They also want to know about your services, but they don't want to be "sold". I know I hate that when someone does it to me!

So, in light of this, here are some words that you should NEVER use with a client ...

"No" - Everyone hates this word!!! It's negative and conveys failure. Try saying "What I can do is this ..." instead. Also, never say "I don't know." Tell them "Let me find out for you".

Here's my customer service policy summed up in a few words ... under promise and over deliver. Respect your client's time, feelings and opinions, but most of all treat your customers like you would like to be treated. Customer service should always come first, no matter what.

Unhappy Clients

At some point, you are eventually going to get an unhappy client. It happens to all of us. You're going to get them once in a while. So here are a few tips on how to handle them when they come across your path.

Remember, if you irritate one client, they'll tell one hundred people about their bad experience, but if you handle the situation right, then they will tell 10 people how wonderful your company is. This is why it is so important to maintain a warm and positive relationship with all your clients.

Listen. Don't interrupt and let them talk it out. We all want people to pay attention to us in this "it's all about me" world that we live in, so pay attention to them and listen! Let them vent their anger and frustration. Quite often, just letting them vent is enough to diffuse the situation because it makes them feel better.

Ask questions. Your first priority is to figure out what the problem is, so ask questions. Clarity is the key here. It also shows that you really care about solving their problem.

Apologize. You absolutely don't want them to think you're giving them a "company policy" answer. You want to personalize it and make them feel special. If they are standing in front of you, then walk over to them, look them in the eyes, and really listen to their problem. Then, immediately let them know that you completely understand their frustration and tell them that you understand how upset they must be. Then say how sorry you are that it happened to them. Tell them that you want to help solve their problem and will do everything possible to help them.

Solve the problem. Call who you need to call and get an answer for the client fast.

Remember, their problem is very important to them! So even if you think that their problem is not important, you must still respect them. Treat everyone you meet with the respect and dignity that they deserve. If you were standing there, how would you want to be treated? What would you want the person to say to you?

Competition

I can't tell you how many phone calls we get about this topic. It's number one on everyone's list ... who is the competition? How do I beat them? They're going to take all the clients!!!

NOT TRUE. There is plenty of business out there for everyone folks.

Let's take a look at the realtors in your town. How many are there? I'll bet you that, for the most part, none of them are stepping on each other's toes and that there is plenty of business for them all. One company couldn't possibly handle all the business in one town as they would be overwhelmed and would soon be out of business. Trust me on this one ... this has happened to a few clients of mine. They were one of the only concierge in town to advertise their business, and WHAM! It worked!! However, they soon became overwhelmed with all the business and had to close down for a few months while they re-organized. Clearly one company can't possibly handle all the business.

Here's another way to look at it ... what would McDonalds be if Burger King hadn't come on the scene??

Wendy's? Taco Bell?

Think they spend their time sending each other hate mail?? I was first! You can't set up your restaurant! It was my idea!!!

See my point? PLENTY of business for everyone. One town can certainly handle more than one company offering the same basic services with no problem at all.

I think competition is good for the soul. It forces us to do better and offer a better product. I also firmly believe in building relation-ships and working together towards the common good. Working together will get us farther than working apart.

And yes ... I practice what I preach. I've actually trained a few of my competitors (although I'll admit I didn't know it at the time) and have even given them some referrals. Should I get mad every time someone publishes another book on the Concierge industry? No ... because it's a big world out there and there is plenty of business for everyone. I think the more books out there on the subject, the better!

My advice to everyone is to bless your competition, shake their hand and welcome them to the neighborhood. Say positive things about them and build a relationship with them. Don't judge them for what they do or not do. Instead, greet them warmly and let them be.

Now why would I want to do that? You might be thinking as you read this.

Good question ... one reason might be that it's the last thing they'll expect you to do. It will certainly shock them for a minute!

The real reason is this ... there is a universal principle that states what you put out into the world will bounce back at you like a boomerang. I know that you've all heard this one. Well, if you put out honesty, integrity, love and respect they will bounce right back at you and will only make your business better and more prosperous. If you put out jealousy, anger, fear and hatred then please learn to duck because it's coming right back at you. Treat your competition as you yourself would like to be treated.

Love will always get you farther than hate.

The most remarkable thing about my mother is that for thirty years she served the family nothing but leftovers. The original meal has never been found.

Calvin Trillin

Chapter 15

The Media and Press Releases

It is an excellent idea to send out a press release to all the local media agencies once you have your new concierge service department established. A truly GREAT way to get some free advertising! A good newspaper article will give you some great free advertising!

Also, you could be a guest on a local radio or television talk show! Think of the free press you would get there!!

On the following pages are two sample press releases. The first is from my own company, and the second is from the International Concierge and Errand Association. Both releases have gotten interviews in varying degrees from newspapers and various other media outlets around the country. When you are ready to send your press release out, just visit www.PRWeb.com and you'll be all set. Fabulous website.

Now, here are a few media tips to help you when you land that interview ...

1. I know very few media people who have the time to listen to your entire story. So I would prepare a 30-second elevator speech that will capture their attention. In 30 seconds or less, tell them why your story will make their show the best it's been in years.

2. Follow-up – Follow-up with everyone. No exceptions. Also return your e-mails and telephone calls within 24 hours or less. Again, no exceptions. If the press can't get you to respond fast, they will simply move on to someone else and you'll lose the interview.

3. Believe – Believe in what you are doing! You can't promote something if you don't believe in it with all your heart. Speak with passion!!

4. Headlines – Make the headlines on your press releases attention grabbers … they should literally reach out and grab them and make them want to read the story. The headline should be short, no more than one line.

5. Word of Mouth – Tell everyone you know what you are doing!! Network, Network, Network!!! Bring your business cards with you absolutely everywhere because you never know who you are going to bump into.

6. Don't look at the camera! If you get interviewed on television, don't look at the camera, look at the person doing the interview.

7. Don't wear white – Also, try and keep your clothing conservative. Women should keep their jewelry and makeup to a minimum.

8. Don't be a "talking head" – Try and talk in short sentences. Don't be long winded!!! Short bursts of information.

9. The camera might be on! Even if you are not talking, the camera might be on you so make sure you control your facial expressions.

10. Be positive and upbeat! Put yourself in a positive mood before the interview!!

11. Nothing is ever "off the record" so don't even go there with a reporter.

12. NEVER say that you don't know, or that you can't answer a question. Change to another topic, or just say when you have an answer for that question, that the reporter will be the first one you call. If you can't answer the question due to a legal problem, then tell them that.

13. No news outlet is too small. Small, medium or large ... it's all good!!!

14. Don't eat a heavy meal before the interview because it will make you tired. Also, don't drink too much liquid, I'm sure I don't have to tell you why!

On the following page, you'll find two sample press releases for you to use as a guide when creating your own. Once finished, you can submit them to your local media as well as www.PRWeb.com.

For more information on PR, you can read *Full Frontal PR* by Richard Laermer. A terrific book that I highly reccommend.

SAMPLE PRESS RELEASE

Concierge Departments Are Not Just For Hotels Anymore

Wake Forest, NC, April 16, 2006 -- Triangle Concierge, Inc. is one of the first companies of its kind in the world today. Headquartered in Wake Forest, NC, Katharine Giovanni, President, works with both individuals and companies all over the world from over 40 countries including Australia, the Middle East, S. Africa and England in ad dition to their many U.S. clients. The company teaches individuals how to start their own concierge service through Giovanni's best-selling book The Concierge Manual, group workshops and individualized one-on-one intense training sessions. In addition, they also provide on-site customized training and consulting services to companies around the world that wish to create in-house concierge departments as a benefit to their employees as well as helping established businesses add a new concierge service division.

The word "concierge" has been in the hotel industry for decades, and has only recently emerged into the corporate world. Concierge businesses and departments are popping up all over the world. There is a huge demand for these kinds of services because more and more people have less and less time to do the things they need to do without interfering with their personal time, let alone work hours. In fact, companies and individuals are not only starting to use concierges, but many are making them a part of their corporate benefit packages. Concierge are now everywhere … from shopping malls to universities, churches, associations, small and large companies, country clubs, condominiums, office buildings and yacht clubs to name just a few.

With a concierge service, individuals become more productive at work when they do not have to come in late or leave early to pick-up dry cleaning and prescriptions, wait for home repairmen and accomplish a host of other necessary and time-consuming evils. Concierge's run office errands, deliver lunch, relocate employees, make travel plans, and plan meetings all at the same time. It is a one-stop shop for virtually anything a person can use.

Triangle Concierge started as a local concierge service targeting corporate clients. Ten years ago, Giovanni was one of the very few concierge service providers in Raleigh, North Carolina. But she was not the first. She was, however, the first in her area to create a website for her company. What happened next should be an example to all of us. People from around the world started contacting Katharine to get information on how she operated her business and get tips on how to start and operate their own concierge business. After getting dozens of calls, Ron (Katharine's business partner and husband) thought it was time to develop a concierge consulting business.

Within months, they began building their concierge consulting business. This included writing her book on how to start a concierge business and marketing herself as a speaker and consultant. "Today, Ron and I have consulted thousands of people from all over the world, and now we are helping corporations start their own in-house concierge departments" says Giovanni. "We are one of the only companies in the world that do what we do. Medical and legal professionals have been specializing for years. Financial consultants help you grow your money, now we have concierge that help you add time to your life. They allow you to squeeze 36 hours into a 24 hour day. In short, Concierge and Lifestyle Management Companies are purveyors of time."

Giovanni is also president of XPACS (www.goxpacs.com), a national concierge company as well as the co-founder of the International Concierge and Errand Association (www.ICEAWeb.org).

If you would like more information on this topic, or to schedule an interview with Katharine Giovanni, please call Katharine at 919-453-2850, or you may email her via her websites at www.triangleconcierge.com www.katharinegiovanni.com.

SAMPLE PRESS RELEASE

Chicago To Host International Concierge and Errand Pros from ICEA

From August 2-5, Concierge and errand business owners from around the world will be converging in Chicago to attend the 5th Annual conference of the International Concierge and Errand Association (ICEA). ICEA is an International Association that supports over 475 concierge and errand service businesses around the world.

Philadelphia, PA (PRWEB) June 8, 2006 – From August 2-5, Concierge and errand business owners from around the world will be converging in Chicago to attend the 5th Annual conference of the International Concierge and Errand Association (ICEA). ICEA is an International Association that supports over 475 concierge and errand service businesses around the world. The conference is open to all members, non-members, suppliers and those considering starting a concierge or errand service business.

"We've seen a dramatic increase in membership every year," says ICEA Interim President, Katharine Giovanni. "Though our members have regular discussions online, this is a great chance for everyone to meet face to face and delve a bit deeper into the issues unique to our industry," she adds. This year's program, "Charting Your Course", features seminars in Sales & Marketing, Contracts

& Proposals, Websites & E-commerce, Business Development, Vendor Management and Start-up Guidance. There are three tracks this year ... one for industry veterans, those in the developing stages and another for industry beginners. Internationally recognized speakers include the VP of Business Development from Constant Contact, Alec Stern, corporate consultant and image specialist Susan Fignar of Pur*Sue, best-selling author Tracy Lynn Moland ("Mom Management") and Concierge Training Expert, Katharine Giovanni of Triangle Concierge, who was recently named ICEA Interim President. ICEA is also proud to have Constant Contact and Mainline Tickets as sponsors for the event as well as vendors from the insurance, credit card and product and service industries.

ICEA is the leading global community for concierge and errand business professionals, serving as the primary resource and active advocate for members by providing essential resources, continuing education, networking opportunities, and other professional endeavors.

Contact:
Carla Mandell
2006 Conference Co-Chair
800-934-ICEA / 215-743-5618

Never be afraid to try something new. Remember that a
lone amateur built the Arc. A large group of professionals
built the Titanic.

Dave Barry

Chapter 16

Nothing Ventured, Nothing Gained

Taking chances.

That seems to be a universal business theme.

Taking chances …

Taking the chance that hiring you will be the perfect solution.

Taking the chance that investing in your company will be a wise investment.

Taking the chance that starting up a company of your own will bring you prosperity.

Taking a chance when the world is telling you the opposite.

This reminds me of an old story my father told me when I was a child …

Years ago, my father worked for a bank in New York City and was approached by someone who offered him some stock in a brand new company. He immediately went to his father and asked him if he thought the investment was wise. My grandfather took one look at the company and told my father that a restaurant who offers only one food choice would never fly, and advised him to not invest in a company that had no future. No one would eat there because people wanted choices. The market wouldn't support it. So Dad took his father's advice and never invested in the company.

Would you like to know the company name?

Kentucky Fried Chicken.

<SIGH>

My father kicked himself over that for years.

Taking chances. Yes, there's a risk. There's ALWAYS a risk! I won't argue that point with you. Life's a risk. Not doing it is also a risk.

So what to do?

Take a deep breath and trust what your intuition is telling you. My father's intuition told him to invest, and he let his brain (and my grandfather) talk him out of something his intuition was guiding him to do.

Trust.

I've told dozens and dozens of clients that the key to business is intuition and persistence. Trusting your intuition to guide you in the right direction, and persistence to KEEP GOING!

DON'T GIVE UP!

If you wish to be successful then I would certainly take a hard look at your business, your services, your market, your fee structure and your sales strategy. However, I would also take a look at what you're thinking.

How you are talking to yourself? If you keep saying things like "I will be successful" or "I will get that investor to invest" then you will be left willing and your success will remain in the future.

Turn your thoughts into the present tense. I AM successful! I have plenty of clients!!! I have plenty of investors!

If you had $100,000 in the bank right now ... what would you be thinking? How would you be conducting your life? Your business? Why wait? Think that way now.

I am not suggesting that you go out and buy a fancy sports car and a million dollar mansion on credit. I am merely pointing out that you should THINK that you can do these things if you want to.

THINK prosperous and you will BE prosperous because if you change the inside, then your world will change on the outside.

Ok, let me say that one again ... this time in a bold font ...

Change the inside and you will change the outside.

Take a chance!

Take a chance to live your passion!

What have you got to lose?

Money? You can always get more of that.

Time? Every morning you're given 24 brand new hours to work with and there's more where that came from. Every sunrise is your chance to start over and make a new choice.

People? People come and go in your life like the tide. Some are meant to be there forever, and some are there to teach you something (or for you to teach them) and then it's time for them to leave. Your real friends will always stand by your side no matter what.

A place? You can always get a new place just like you can always buy new things.

So I'll ask you again. What have you got to lose?

Take the chance.

Take the chance to do it … or to not do it. Just take the chance.

Life is about taking chances. You can have everything you've ever dreamed of! All you have to do is take the chance.

As they say … nothing ventured, nothing gained.

 **Chapter 17**

Half Empty or Half Full? It's up to you!

How you look at the world will directly affect your business bottom line. Your inside world will directly affect your outside world. How you talk to yourself, and how you view the world either positively or negatively direclty affects how you live, how you think and what you do.

I'll never forget what the late Peter Jennings said one night a few years ago. He looked directly into the camera and said *"the mind body relationship is serious science."* Very true. The mind can heal the body with a thought, or the mind can squash a business deal with a doubt. Serious science.

To illustrate this idea, allow me to tell you a little story.

A few years ago, I took my boys to the neighborhood pool. They were excited because the pool had just opened for the season. When we got there, I quickly found some chairs near some acquaintances of ours, and as the boys swam, we started to chat.

About 20 minutes went by when I began to notice that everything my friend talked about had a negative slant to it. First it was complaining about a particular teacher at school, then it was about the lack of time in life in general, and on and on it went. She said nothing positive … all negative, complaining about this and that. When she got to politics, I decided that it was enough and quickly excused myself and jumped into the pool.

As I swam around the pool, I couldn't help but hear other conversations. Imagine my surprise when I found that they too were mostly negative!!! Curious now, I walked over to the soda machine and said, *"how are you?"* to some other neighbors. Their reply? *"Tired. You know how it goes."* Not exactly negative, but certainly not positive either.

So now I was REALLY curious! Was it just that it was the end of the week and everyone was tired and grumpy? I decided to test it, so for the next few days I really paid attention to everything I saw and heard to see how much negativity there really was in the world.

I have to say that I didn't have to try very hard.

First, I went to the grocery store. As I waited for the clerk to tally my groceries, I started chatting with her and soon I was being told a story about when she was in Japan. Since she has blond hair, she complained that her trip was horrible because all the Japanese wanted to do was touch it.

That evening I switched on the evening news and was presented with 30 minutes of rape, murder, robberies, drownings and child abductions. In between these heartwarming stores, I listened to commercials about weight loss, adult ADD and a new drug that they said everyone should take (but had some small side effects like nausea and sometimes death).

Alrighty then!!!

After the news, I flipped around and found more heartwarming stores on television such as "Law and Order," "ER" and "CSI Miami". All great shows but hardly positive. It seems I was surrounded by murder, rape and the dregs of society - all in primetime! I settled for a "Touched by an Angel" rerun and went to bed.

When I woke up the next morning, I continued to pay attention.

The first thing on my agenda that morning was a visit to the post office. As I drove, I flipped on the radio to my favorite radio station and what do I hear? I hear a woman singing the following lyrics ... *"wounds won't seem to heal, the pain is just too real."* I switched to another station.

At the post office I was greeted at the door by an identity theft poster. I then went to our local Target store to pick up a new bathing suit for one of my sons and noticed that they had TV monitors all over the place. As I looked at one, I saw a story about how to prevent your child from being abducted.

Are you seeing a pattern here? I promise you that I'm not making this up.

Ok ... let's try the computer. Maybe that's better.

After logging on, I took a look at my homepage at MSN and saw a story about Al-Qaida, another about a woman found strangled, and a weather related story about a nasty tornado.

Let's not forget my e-mail. I had my usual number of SPAM emails, which generally include sales pitches, porn and various offers about Viagra. Oh ... don't forget the one from Nigeria who wants to wash one million dollars through my bank account. Of course he'll give me half.

Uh huh. I totally believe you.

Later that day, I went to get my mail and saw my neighbor outside doing some yard work. When I stopped to say hello he asked me how I was doing. So I replied *"No worries mate, I'm doing really great today!"* (I just love that Australian expression). I really don't think he was expecting me to say that because he stopped what he was doing and looked at me like I had just escaped from an insane asylum. I just laughed, told him I would see him later and went into my house.

When did it become politically incorrect to tell people something positive?

I have to tell you all that by the end of the second day I was incredibly tired. So tired I went to bed at 9:00 p.m. and asked my husband Ron to put the boys to bed. I just wanted to lie down and pull the covers way up over my head and forget about it all.

So what did I learn from this little test? I learned that you can mess up your mind with this stuff! I felt like I had been dragged into a negative world filled with greed, fear and hatred. A world where you always lack money and never achieve your life's dreams because you're too fat, too thin, too sick, going to be sick, need a job, lost a job, and on and on it seemed to go.

I felt that my brain had been so saturated with negativity that I was in danger of becoming physically sick! By the end of the second day I was yelling at my kids, bickering with my husband and grumpy to everyone.

So I had a huge bowl of ice cream (which I'm convinced cures every-thing), took a hot bath and went to bed. The test was officially over. Two days was more than enough for me.

On the third day, I decided to visit the same places I had gone during the last two days to see what positives I could find there. First, I went to the pool and sat down in a chair. As I watched, I saw people laugh-ing and smiling, and children playing in the pool with huge smiles on their face. The sound of happy children playing is really one of life's greatest sounds and put an immediate smile on my face.

I then went to the grocery store to pick up some milk, and saw aisle after aisle filled with food, supplies, drinks and fresh produce. Now here was abundance and prosperity! I saw people chatting and smil-ing, and two children happily eating a messy chocolate doughnut.

I went back to the Post Office and started to chat with the woman in front of me who was mailing a package to her son in Iraq filled with things she thought he might need.

I logged onto the Internet and received a wonderful e-mail from a friend entitled "The Positive Side of Life." I then received an e-mail from an old friend of mine whom I've known since I was three years old (we won't say how long that is!). It always puts a smile on my face when I hear from her.

As I was leaving the house to pick up my boys from school, I saw my neighbor again. So I asked him how he was doing. He turned and looked at me with a big smile on his face and replied *"No worries mate!"* As I drove away, I flipped on the radio and immediately heard a song called "I'm on Top of the World!"

That evening, I turned on the evening news, and heard an extremely beautiful story about a woman moving into her first home - built by the wonderful organization Habitat for Humanity. Then the weather came on and I was told that bright sunshine would be in our area for the next few days. Later that evening, I watched a rerun from that great show on ABC called *Extreme Makeover Home Edition.* In seven days they completely change a needy family's home and life. What an act of kindness!

Now there is a natural law out there called the Law of Focus. Simply put, this law states that what you put your attention to grows. Certainly the case here! I put my attention to all the negative "stuff" in the world and it slammed into me so hard that I wanted to cry from the pain. It got so bad that I saw it everywhere I went. From the grocery store to the post office to my own home. It could make a person seriously paranoid and horribly sick. When I placed my attention on the positive, it grew too. It was like it had suddenly stopped raining and the warm sun came out.

So how do you remain positive, healthy and prosperous in a negative world? Here's what I do ...

1. Surround yourself with positive people. Treat others like you want to be treated ... positively! With positive encouragement and thoughts!!!

2. TURN OFF THE NEWS as much as possible.

3. Try and avoid newspapers ... although you should scan the headlines so that you know what's going on in the world.

4. Write down all the positive things that have happened to you in the last month and post them where you can see them. "See" your life as a success!!! Don't "see" your life as a failure!!! Look at all the positive things that you've done!!!

5. Put a positive/inspirational poster over your desk. You can also put a "plus" sign, or the words "stay positive" over your desk to remind you to be positive.

6. Read some inspirational books like the one from my friend, Connie Domino, called *Develop Irresistible Attraction.*

7. Turn someone else's negative day into a positive and help them out!

Now please know that I'm not telling you to blindly ignore the reality of the world. I'm telling you that you can see that reality and also see the POSITIVES as well. The world can indeed be a cruel place. Crime, poverty and illness seem to be everywhere ... but the world can be a beautiful place filled with love, warmth, compassion and prosperity.

Do you see the glass as half-full or half-empty?

Negative things will happen in the world. They happen to all of us!

But look at it this way ... positive things will happen as well. Good things will happen to you. Joy will find you!

It goes back to the law of physics

1. Every action causes a reaction

2. We attract like energy

So if we put out negative thoughts and actions and constantly focus on the negative, we will ATTRACT negative back to us. It will be all that we see!! Conversely, if we put out positive thoughts and try our best to see the positive, then we will attract the positive back.

We live in a negative world. So be it. However, I refuse to be negative and will continue to remain positive as much as possible. I've had my share of bad times, trust me, I wrote the book on that one. The good news is that I don't have to stay that way if I don't choose to. I choose prosperity, love and compassion. I choose to look at the glass as half full, one day at a time.

In conclusion, in order to become a successful concierge what do you need to do?

You need to do whatever it takes.

"Whatever it takes" - an incredible group of words when you think about it.

I'll do whatever it takes.

To what?

Whatever it takes to become a success? Whatever it takes to lose the weight? Whatever it takes to pay my bills? Even if it means giving something up?

I was watching Oprah the other day, and was told a story about two young men who saw an oil tanker go off the road right in front of them. As the truck burst into flames, they pulled their car over and without thinking ran down the embankment, raced through the flames, and pulled the driver out to safety. Seconds after they pulled him out the truck exploded. The amazing part was that they did it without thinking! They told Oprah it never occurred to them to not do it, they simply saw a man in need and reacted. She just sat there in awe.

Whatever it takes.

Personally, I've lived by this mantra for years. I've done whatever it took to get our company up and running with no budget. Whatever it took to get my mother help when she was sick, whatever it took to help our neighbors when they were in need.

It never occurred to me to NOT run into the fire when someone or something needed me ... I just did it without thought.

I've also been known to do whatever it takes to BELIEVE that I can do whatever it takes.

My husband Ron does whatever it takes. A few summers ago, he ran into a nasty undertow to save someone from drowning. He saw the lifeguard race into the water and instinctively ran in after him. He also saved two people from choking to death when he was in his twenties. He's done this sort of thing a lot over the years. It's who he is.

Whatever it takes ... no matter what the topic.

So do whatever it takes to become a success in your new business!

Do whatever it takes to be kind, loving, generous and warm.

Do whatever it takes to help someone out.

Do whatever it takes to spend time with your family.

How much should you do? How hard should you work?

Just do whatever it takes.

Until next time everyone,

Katharine

We're here for a reason. I believe a bit of the reason is to throw little torches out to lead people through the dark.

Whoopi Goldberg

Chapter 18

Helpful Books and Websites

The Concierge Industry

www.triangleconcierge.com - International Concierge Consultants offering books, live workshops, concierge software and more!

www.ICEAWeb.org - The International Concierge and Errand Association (ICEA) . ICEA is an International Association that provides assistance to concierge and errand services around the world. The association offers members networking opportunities, continuing education, books, software and industry recognition.

Start Your Own Personal Concierge Service (Entrepreneur Magazine's Start Ups) by Entrepreneur Press (*please wait for the 2006/2007 version. It's MUCH better and more up-to-date. The 2003 version is dated*)

http://messageboards.ivillage.com/iv-wferrand- iVillage Errand Service Message Board.

http://groups.yahoo.com/group/conciergenet/- Yahoo Concierge Board.

http://finance.groups.yahoo.com/group/errand_services -- Yahoo Errand Service board.

Business Information

The Consultant's Guide to Proposal Writing: How to Satisfy Your Clients and Double Your Income by Herman Holtz.

Weekend Entrepreneur: 101 Great Ways to Earn Extra Cash by Michelle Anton, Jennifer Basye

Business Plans Kit For Dummies by Steven D. Peterson, Peter E. Jaret, Barbara Findlay Schenck

www.allbusiness.com - AllBusiness.com is a one-stop resource for expert advice on growing and managing your business

www.irs.treas.gov - U.S. Internal Revenue Service.

http://taxmama.com - Tax Information With A Mother's Touch.

www.sba.gov - Small Business Association.

www.score.org - Service Corps of Retired Executives.

http://www.entrepreneur.com - great business website from Entrepreneur Magazine.

http://www.logoyes.com/ - Create your own logo!

www.vistaprint.com - VistaPrint.com is the Web's innovative e-printing site that lets you easily customize and order your own FREE, high-quality, full-color business cards. They're great cards.

BigDates.com - BigDates is an extremely helpful tool for Concierges, and it takes just a few minutes to set up. It helps you remember and take action on the 'BIG DATES' in your client's lives, like birthdays, anniversaries, and holidays. It reminds you via email or cell phone and suggests appropriate greeting cards and gifts.

http://sbinfocanada.about.com/library/startbusinessquiz/blquestion1. htm - Many people dream of starting a business, but are hesitant to start a business of their own. Are you one of those people wondering if starting a business is right for you? This starting a business quiz will help you decide whether or not the time is right for you to start your own business.

http://www.xe.com/ucc/ - The Universal Currency Converter®.

http://decoder.americom.com/?clkd=iwm - Area Code Decoder. I use this all the time if I don't recognize the area code and need to know what time zone they are in before I return the call.

http://www.timeanddate.com - Tells you what time it is all over the world.

http://www.about.com - Has a lot of useful information.

http://www.findlaw.com - Research legal issues. The section "for legal professionals" is also available to the general public.

http://www.melissadata.com - demographics research site.

http://www.city-data.com - demographics research site for public information.

http://www.toolkit.cch.com/ - lots of good information in here!

Customer Service

Integrity Service: Treat Your Customers Right-Watch Your Business Grow by Ron Willingham

Neon Signs of Service by Holly Stiel

Professional Impressions ... Etiquette for Everyone, Every Day by Marjorie Brody

Superior Customer Service: How to Keep Customers Racing Back to Your Business--Time Tested Examples from Leading Companies by Dan W. Blacharski

Public Relations, The Media, Newsletters

Full Frontal PR by Richard A. Laermer

The Publicity Handbook, New Edition : The Inside Scoop from More than 100 Journalists and PR Pros on How to Get Great Publicity Coverage by David R. Yale, Andrew J. Carothers

Publicityinsider.com - PR Tips, Press Release Secrets, and the Inside Track to Huge Publicity.

http://www.prweb.com/ - free online press release distribution services.

http://www.prleap.com - Free Press Release Distribution

http://www.ezinequeen.com - If you're an independent professional or small business owner, one of the most proven ways to attract new business is to gain status as an expert or resource in your field. One of the easiest, cheapest, and most effective ways to do this is to publish an e-mail newsletter, or "e-zine." Has some great free tips and articles on her site.

http://ezinearticles.com/ - A great site if you need some articles for your newsletter.

www.press-release-writing.com - Writing a Press Release with tips, examples, and a template.

International Protocal

Global Business Etiquette: A Guide to International Communication and Customs by Jeanette S. Martin and Lillian H. Chaney

http://www.kwintessential.co.uk - If you are doing business overseas, or you need to purchase a gift for someone outside of the United States, it is important to know their culture so that you can't make a mistake. This website is absolutely wonderful! Click on "Country Profiles" in their resource section and you'll learn everything you need to know about that particular country including information on business etiquette and what gifts to buy and not buy. A really great resource.

http://www.executiveplanet.com - from their website: "Executive Planet™ provides valuable tips on business etiquette, customs and protocol for doing business worldwide. Our guides are co-authored by experts in international business etiquette, who are available to answer your questions on the discussion board."

http://babelfish.altavista.com/tr - are you working with an international client? Need something translated? This site is great and will translate any language.

Meeting/Event Planning

If you are planning on offering Meeting and Event Planning, then I suggest you visit Meeting Professionals International at www. mpiweb.org.

Life and Time Management

Develop Irresistible Attraction By Connie Domino - www.Connie-Domino.com

Spiritual Marketing: A Proven 5-Step Formula for Easily Creating Wealth from the Inside Out by Joe Vitale and Bob Proctor

Spiritual Economics: The Principles and Process of True Prosperity by Eric Butterworth

Rich Dad, Poor Dad: What the Rich Teach Their Kids About Money--That the Poor and Middle Class Do Not! by Robert T. Kiyosaki, Sharon L. Lechter

Money is My Friend for the New Millenium, Second Edition by Phil Laut, Jeffrey Combs

9 Steps to Financial Freedom: Practical and Spiritual Steps So You Can Stop Worrying; Revised and Updated Version by Suze Orman

Think and Grow Rich by Napoleon Hill

Time Management from the Inside Out by Julie Morgenstern. Henry Holt

First Things First: To Live, to Love, to... by Stephen R. Covey, A. Roger Merrill, and Rebecca R. Merrill

Mompreneurs: A Mother's Practical Step by Step Guide to Work at Home Success by Patricia Cobe and Ellen H. Parlapiano

Mom Management™ by Tracy Lynn Moland - http://www.tracylynmoland.com

How to Make the Rest of Your Life the Best of Your Life by Mark Victor Hansen and Art Linkletter

The Power of Focus: How to Hit Your Business, Personal and Financial Targets with Absolute Certainty by Jack Canfield

Bibliography

1. Zig Ziglar's Secrets of Closing the Sale, Zig Ziglar, Berkley
    Books, New York 1984.

2. The Contract and Fee-Setting Guide for Consultants and
    Professionals, Howard L. Shenson, John Wiley & Sons, Inc.,
    New York 1990.

3. Selling your Services to the Meeting's Market, Bill Quain,
    Ph.D., Meeting Professionals International, 1993.

4. The Meeting Planner's Guide to Logistics and Arrangements,
    Stanley Mark Wolfson, Institute for Meeting and Conference
    Management, Washington DC, 1986.

5. Entrepreneur Magazine's "Concierge Services," http://www.
    entrepreneurmag.com/entmag/hotbiz99/concierge.html

6. Entrepreneur Magazine's "Personal Concierge Services,"
    http://www.entrepreneurmag.com/startup/topbiz99/personal.
    html

7. Entrepreneur Magazine's "Senior Concierge Services," http://
    www.entrepreneurmag.com/startups/bsu_top10.hts

8. Entrepreneur Magazine's "Now Serving," http://www.entrepre-
    neurmag.com/page.hts?N=6805

9. Entrepreneur Magazine's "Consider it Done," http://www. entrepreneurmag.com/page.hts?N=5383

10. http://www.errandinfo.com

11. Full Frontal PR, Richard A. Laermer, Bloomberg Press, Princ eton, NJ, 2003.

Stubbornness is also determination. It's simply a matter
of shifting from "won't power" to "will power."

Peter McWilliams

Appendix

Sample Forms and Applications

On the next few pages you will find some helpful forms and applications that some of my clients have used. As I've said before, there are almost 10,000 ways to do this, these forms are merely an example of one. You really can do these yourself.

Also included is a very simple business plan for you to use as a guide when you create your own.

Lastly, a sample employee handbook has been added for you to use when your company grows to the point of actually hiring employees.

Good luck!

Sample Employment Application

(For employees without a resume)

Personal Information

First Name:_____

Middle Initial: _____

Last Name: _____

Address:_____

City, State, Zip Code: _____

Home Telephone: (   ) _____

Work Telephone: (   ) _____

E-mail Address:_____

Social Security Number: _____

Date of Birth: _____

Date of availability for employment: _____

Have you ever been arrested?   (   ) yes   (   ) no

If yes, please explain: _____

_____

Education

1. Name and address of School, Business School, College/University:

_____

Years attended: _____

Degree: _____

2. Name and address of School, Business School, College/University:

_____

Years attended: _____

Degree: _____

3. Name and address of School, Business School, College/University:

_____

Years attended: _____

Degree: _____

Special Training:

Please include Military, Certificates, Specific Courses, Correspondence Schools, Adult Education, etc.

   1. School or Agency: _____
        Subject: _____
        Length of Training: _____

   2. School or Agency: _____
        Subject: _____
        Length of Training: _____

   3. School or Agency: _____
        Subject: _____
        Length of Training: _____

Work Experience:

May we contact your present employer? (   ) yes   (   ) no

1.   Employed from (month/year): _____ to _____

Name of Employer: _____

Supervisor's Name: _____

Address: _____

City/State/Zip Code: _____

Telephone Number: (   ) _____

Job Title: _____

Job Duties: (continue on separate paper if necessary)

_____

_____

_____

Reason for Leaving: (continue on separate paper if necessary)

_____

_____

2.   Employed from (month/year): _____ to _____

Name of Employer: _____

Supervisor's Name: _____

Address: _____

City/State/Zip Code: _____

Telephone Number: (   ) _____

Job Title: _____

Job Duties: (continue on separate paper if necessary)

_____

_____

_____

Reason for Leaving: (continue on separate paper if necessary)

_____

_____

3.   Employed from (month/year): _____ to _____

Name of Employer: _____

Supervisor's Name: _____

Address: _____

City/State/Zip Code: _____

Telephone Number: (   ) _____

Job Title: _____

Job Duties: (continue on separate paper if necessary)

_____

_____

_____

Reason for Leaving: (continue on separate paper if necessary)

_____

_____

_____

Thank you

Sample Client Application

(Should be printed on your own letterhead)

Full Name: _____

Nickname: _____

Company Name: _____

Title: _____

Address: _____

City: _____State ____ Zip Code: _____

Work Phone number: (   ) _____

Fax number: (   ) _____

E-mail Address: _____

Home Address: _____

City: _____State ____ Zip Code: _____

Home Telephone: (   ) _____

Personal Information:

Date of Birth: _____

Marital Status: ( ) single   ( ) married

Spouse/Significant Other

Full Name: _____

Nickname: _____

Date of Birth: _____

Children

Name: _____ Date of Birth: _____
Name: _____ Date of Birth: _____
Name: _____ Date of Birth: _____

Payment Information: Please Check One

_____Check   _____ Credit Card   _____ Concierge Account

Other Interests:

Are there any days that are very important to you? Anniversary? Religious Holidays? Family member's birthday? Special holidays?

Do you have pets? How many, what kind?

What are you allergic to? Any food allergies?

What is your favorite flower?

What is your favorite color?

What type events/shows/sporting events do you like?

What are you and your significant other interested in?

What are your children interested in?

Sample Vendor Application

BUSINESS CATEGORY: _____

CONTACT NAME: _____

TITLE: _____

COMPANY: _____

ADDRESS: _____

CITY, STATE, ZIP CODE: _____

TELEPHONE: (   ) _____

FAX: (   ) _____

E-MAIL: _____

WEBPAGE: _____

DESCRIPTION OF SERVICES:

_____

_____

_____

_____

_____

_____

<u>REFERENCES:</u>

Please give us the names of three clients (either current or within the past six months).

Name: _____

Address: _____

Telephone Number: (   ) _____

Name: _____

Address: _____

Telephone Number: (   ) _____

Name: _____

Address: _____

Telephone Number: (   ) _____

Please attach your company brochure and business card so that we may add it to our files.

THANK YOU!

Sample Vendor Proposal

Date

Mr. Stan Vendor
727 ABC Road
Charlotte, NC 33333

Dear Stan:

As per our recent telephone conversation, Sample Concierge would like to add your business services to our member Business Referral List.

In short, we are Sample City's new personal assistant and meeting/event/travel planner. We are dedicated to giving our clients back one of their most valuable possessions…time. Rather than spend part of their busy workday ordering flowers, planning vacations, checking airfares, ordering transportation (train, plane, bus, limousine), ordering tickets or leaving early to pick up dry cleaning and groceries you can now call us to do these tiresome tasks for you. Sample Concierge is a one-stop shop where you can send us your "to do" list and then consider it done!

Our **Business Referral Service** works like this… Clients are more than welcome to access our business referral service and obtain a referral for virtually anything. Business such as Childcare, Maids and Cleaning Professionals, Mechanics, Plumbers, Electricians, Realtors, Builders, Architects, Petcare, Landscapers, Wallpaper Hangers, Painters, Carpet Cleaners, Locksmiths, Health and Fitness Clubs, Moving Companies and more.

If you would like to join our business referral list, then please fill out the attached forms and send them to us. We ask for a reasonable 10% commission for every referral we send you, but don't worry if your business is not set up for this. As part of our services to our clients we always follow up with them to find out if they were completely satisfied with the vendors that we referred them to. This helps us to provide the very best to our clients, plus it keeps our best vendors at the top of our referral list.

If you wish to check us out then please visit our website at www. sampleconcierge.com. You can also call us at 333-123-4567. Thank you and I look forward to hearing from you soon.

    Sincerely,

    Joseph Van Pelt
    President

Sample Driver Trip Sheet

Name:_____   Date: _____
Starting Mileage: _____   Starting Time: _____
Ending Mileage: _____   Ending Time: _____
Gas $_____

Total Reimbursements: _____
Today's Collections: _____

Client Name _____

Name of Store/Address of Home _____

Arrival Time _____

Depart Time _____

Method of Payment Used _____

Total $ _____

Receipt Attached.

Notes:_____

Sample Errand Order Sheet
(Side 1)

Today's Date: _____

Client ID #: _____

Name: _____

Company Name: _____

Pick up from: (   ) Home   (   ) Office

Street Address: _____

Directions: _____

_____

Delivery to: (   ) Home   (   ) Office

Street Address: _____

Directions: _____

_____

Payment via: (   ) Check   (   ) Visa   (   ) Mastercard

Credit Card Number: _____

Expiration Date: _____

Sample Errand Order Sheet
(Side 2)

Errands Needed Done:

1. _____

2. _____

3. _____

4. _____

5. _____

6. _____

7. _____

8. _____

9. _____

10. _____

Customer's signature required upon receipt

Sample Daily Dry Cleaning Trip Sheet

If you don't want to outsource to a dry cleaner who delivers and prefer to do it yourself in-house, then this form might help you.

DATE: _____

Client Name _____

Pick-up Address _____

Store Location _____

Date Dropped Off _____

Date Picked Up _____

Time Delivered to Client _____

Total $ _____

Method of Payment _____

Customer's signature required upon receipt

The following is a sample template form written by Jackie Murphy of EK Errands Express. Although this particular form is more generic and fairly simple, it does give you an example of the great detail she includes in her form templates.

In fact, Jackie has many forms and templates available to help you with your new business that you will find incredibly useful. For more information, and to see some other industry products, please visit www.triangleconcierge.com/bookstore.htm, and click on "other industry products"

BEFORE YOU LEAVE HOME CHECKLIST

(TO BE COMPLETED BY CLIENT & OBTAINED BY SITTER AT FIRST SCHEDULED VISIT)

GENERAL HOME PREPARATION

- ☐ Water plants.
- ☐ Unplug any unnecessary appliances sensitive to power surges (computers, microwaves, television sets).
- ☐ Dial your thermostat up/down for temperature of the season
- ☐ Set water heater temperate down.
- ☐ Stop all home delivery services (mail, newspaper, milk, diapers, etc. if applicable.
- ☐ Arrange for pet care at a kennel or in your home .
- ☐ Mow the lawn if necessary.
- ☐ Visually inspect all windows, screens & check doors are locked.
- ☐ Have window coverings set as you desire.
- ☐ If making duplicate keys, TRY THEM OUT to be sure they work.

- Inform neighbor(s) you have arranged a sitter for your home.
- Give neighbors the name & phone number of sitter in case of emergency.

KITCHEN

- Store food in your freezer to prevent spoilage.
- Clean out & remove perishable items from your refrigerator.
- Empty all waste baskets, put into trash bags and set in garage for trash day.
- Run garbage disposal to eliminate possibility of unpleasant odors.
- Wash dishes or run dishwasher and put dishes away.

PERSONAL PREPARATION

- Schedule a medical check-up before the trip. Ask doctor about necessary vaccinations & have any medical procedures done before you go.
- Take all necessary medications with you.
- Arrange for refills of medications.
- Update any personal identification so it contains current information and photograph.
- Pick up cash, change, and traveler's checks at the bank and put them in a place where you know where they are and are secure.
- Get a telephone calling card and take it with you OR if you have a cell phone, make sure you take your charger.
- Fill out and send in your tax return form if you will be out of town at the deadline or notify your tax preparer of temporary address where you can be reached and forms can be sent for signature.

- ☐ Fill out an absentee voter form if you will be out of town at election time.
- ☐ Tell your friends/relatives of your address where you can be reached while out-of-town.
- ☐ Pay rent and other bills. If you'll be gone for an extended period of time, pay ahead or arrange for a friend/relative/house sitter to pay the bills.
- ☐ Do laundry so you won't have to worry about it when you return from your trip.
- ☐ Break in new shoes to prevent blisters and pack according to your needs – do not over pack.

SANITY SAVERS

- ☐ Make a "fun bag" for each child and include games, books, toys, a tape player with headphones, and snacks.
- ☐ Pack a cooler with snacks and drinks for yourself if you are driving.
- ☐ Purchase postcard/regular postage stamps and take with you.
- ☐ Print address labels of people to send postcards to. It's much lighter to carry a sheet of labels than your address book or remember to bring your address book.
- ☐ Be sure and pack/take your camera or video camera.

SECURITY

- ☐ Lock all windows and doors securely and remove any keys hidden outside the house.
- ☐ Inform your neighbors you'll be away and you have a house-sitter coming.
- ☐ Turn on telephone answering machine, but do NOT say you are away! You may also want to change the message on your

voicemail at work to let your business contacts know you are unavailable but state when you will be available again.

□ Set lights, radio or TV on timers. You may have the option to set your TV/Radio on a timer to turn on/off but make sure it is set loud enough to be heard outside.

□ Close blinds and curtains so no one can see directly inside.

□ Instruct anyone authorized to come into your home when they leave they should securely lock doors and any other outside accessible areas.

□ Make sure any authorized person to enter your home other than sitter knows they should call sitter to inform them they will be at home. This eliminates sitter being surprised upon arrival and calling the police if someone is there and they did not know someone was going to be there.

□ Give a key to a nearby neighbor as a backup in the event of extreme weather.

□ Advise gate/alarm company that ABC COMPANY will be visiting your home and authorize entry.

□ Create a password for your security company which your sitter can use if the alarm is tripped and advise your sitter of the telephone and password.

HOUSE SITTER INFORMATION:

□ If you prefer your sitter use a garage door opener to enter residence, please also provide her with a house key. During power failures, garage door openers will not work.

□ Instruct sitter of any lights, TV/Radio that are on timers and what lights to rotate if applicable.

□ Make sure your sitter has your address and telephone numbers to reach you while you are away.

□ Make sure your sitter has your neighbors' and/or emergency

contact phone numbers in case needed.
- ☐ Advise sitter of trash day.
- ☐ Advise sitter of alarm company information, code and phone number.
- ☐ Advise sitter of ANYONE who may be on your premises or entering your home during your absence (housekeeper, relatives, friends, etc.)

- ☐ ONE LAST LOOK AROUND TO ASSURE ALL ENTRY WAYS (WINDOWS, GARAGE, AND PATIO DOORS) ARE SECURE AND EVERYTHING IS IN PLACE

- ☐ ENABLE SECURITY ALARM AND DOUBLE CHECK THE EXIT DOOR IS SECURED

- ☐ MAKE SURE YOU HAVE SITTERS NAME AND PHONE NUMBERS WITH YOU

HAVE A GREAT TRIP AND FEEL FREE TO CALL AND CHECK ON YOUR HOME ANYTIME!

Reprinted with Permission from ...

Jackie Murphy
EK Errands Express
Office: (317) 356-4936
Website: www.EK-Errands-Express.com
Email: Jackie@EK-Errands-Express.com

Sample Services Questionnaire (side 1)

Your company is considering offering a concierge service to its employees and would like to know if this type of service would be of value to you. Please take a moment to let us know what you think!

Would you use this type of service?   ___Yes ___No

If so, how often do you think you would call for errand assistance?
         __ not at all   __ once a month __ once a week __ more often

What types of errands do you need handled? (pick three)_____
_____ _____

Are there any services not listed that you would like to see offered?
                        ___ Yes ___ No

If yes, please tell us what they are _____

Would you be inclined to call for a parent or a spouses needs?
                        ___ Yes   ___ No

Please be honest, how much would you expect to pay for this type of timesaver?
                        $_____ per hour

Do you think that a service like this would be beneficial to you?
                        ___ Yes   ___ No

Do you think that you would be more focused at work if you didn't have to worry aout all the tasks you had to take care of after work?
                        ___ Yes   ___ No

Would you like to see this type of service offered as part of a benefits package?
___ Yes   ___ No

We want to know how you feel, please feel free to write down any other comments you many have!_____
_____

Thank you for taking the time to tell us what you think! We really do know how valuable your time is! We look forward to serving you in the future!

Sample Services Questionnaire (side 2)

Services currently offered ...

Personal/Professional Errands

Run errands large and small
Writing letters and meaningful thank you cards
Deliver packages and documents, Post office needs
Visit the hospitalized and deliver clothes, magazines and flowers
Pick up movie or theatre tickets
Dry cleaning pick-up/drop-off
Child care finders
Personal shopper, gift returns, gift wrapping
Shoe repair
Video rentals and/or returns
Motor Vehicle Services
Have keys made
New Move unpacking
Wait for the service man

Business/Executive Services

Concierge services, Meeting coordination
Telephone services, Internet research
Office supplies, Banking services, Printing services, Notary services
File legal documents
Picking up airline tickets, Film drop-off and delivery
Making travel arrangements
Address and mail seasonal greeting cards
Pick up building supplies
We'll even take your dog or cat to the veterinarian or groomer
Wait for delivery or serviceman, verify workmanship, sign off and lock
    up your home
We'll find the perfect gift for your valued client, employee or boss

(Reprinted with permission of Go-Fers Unlimited)

Concierge Sample Job Descriptions

SAMPLE 1

Immediate Opening

Concierge / Personal Assistant

ABC Company has an exciting, entry-level opportunity for a bright, resourceful, detail oriented and deadline driven individual to join our team. Candidate will be responsible for relationship with our Center City client. As Concierge you will assist our members with solutions for the items on their personal "To Do" list including making dinner reservations, finding hard to get tickets, researching products, locating contractors and housecleaners. Concierge will also coordinate with main office any requests for errands, including grocery or gift shopping, auto repairs, and waiting for deliveries. Concierge will assist with publication and distribution of quarterly newsletter and other duties as assigned.

The candidate should have a background in customer service, management or marketing. Candidate should also be well versed in internet navigation. Excellent communication skills, both written and verbal are a must. We will provide necessary training. Candidate should be comfortable working alone. Candidate has opportunity of earning an annual bonus based upon vendor commissions and discounts negotiated. Growth potential exists as we are a start up company.

If interested, please fax or email your resume and salary requirements to _____.

SAMPLE 2

The following job description is to give a general idea of the position and in no way states or implies that these are the only duties to be performed by the concierge.

ABC COMPANY is looking for people who anticipate (and meet) clients' needs. Here at ABC COMPANY, extraordinary service goes way beyond the normal attempts to deliver customer satisfaction and always exceeds customer expectations.

ABC COMPANY is looking for concierge professionals who behave, speak, and conduct themselves in a manner that is befitting to the industry. We require "over the top" customer service and expect all emails and telephone calls to be returned immediately. We expect our Concierge Professionals to be responsible, creative and intelligent individuals who are able to interact with every type of personality. They should be passionate about their work and exhibit an "all the way" or nothing attitude. Whatever needs to be done will get done by the time specified by the client … no matter what.

Since ABC COMPANY client's are extremely high profile people, we are looking for candidates who will treat them as the individuals they are. Star struck individuals need not apply for this position. For example, if a concierge receives a call from Shaquille O'Neal, he should be treated as a normal everyday paying client with a "Yes Mr. O'Neal, what can I do for you today?" He should NOT be treated as "Shaq" from the Lakers with a "Oh Shaq, it's really you!" Concierge cannot interact on any other level than business with clients and their families.

Qualifications:

The candidate should have a background in customer service, management, sales and/or marketing. Hotel concierge experience is helpful but not required. Experience in the Hospitality Industry is helpful, but not required. ABC COMPANY concierges are enthusiastic, positive, polished, poised and extremely professional.

- Must have strong knowledge of the local and surrounding areas and its venues.
- Exemplary customer service ability and experience.
- Client relationship building skills.
- Resourceful with aptitude for research.
- Excellent verbal and written communication skills.
- Excellent telephone etiquette.
- Proven computer skills (word, excel, internet); resourceful and creative.
- Ability to multitask, attention to detail and follow-through.
- Team-player, detail-oriented.
- Proven success in a results-driven environment.
- Excellent negotiation skills.
- Presentation skills to groups of 20+ people.
- Exhibit the ability to work well in a fast-paced enviroment.
- Exhibit the ability to work well under pressure.
- Flexible schedule and willingness to be flexible.

Education and Experience:

Bachelor's degree from 4-year college or university; or one to two years related experience and/or training; or equivalent combination of education and experience. Proficient at using a Windows environment, the Internet, and Microsoft Office Suite.

ABC COMPANY will provide the necessary concierge training.

ABC COMPANY Concierge Duties

ABC COMPANY concierge are responsible for fielding and fulfilling personal requests from clients. Below is a sample of a few of the types of requests.

- Travel and Destination Management
- Restaurant Referral & Preferred Reservations
- Obtain Tickets to Special Events
- Special Date Reminder Service
- Gift Selection
- Shopping Service
- Floral Services – Selection & Delivery
- Limousine Services
- Errand Running
- Meeting and Event Planning
- Recreation Planning, Reservations & Coordination
- Business Support Services
- Home Cleaning Service

Our Concierge Professionals provide the best in Professional and personalized service

Salary and Benefits

Salary is currently being determined. Will be commensurate with experience.

What to Expect at The Interview

Please dress for success.

ABC COMPANY is looking for concierge professionals who are honest, ethical and who will treat our clients in a respectful, friendly and courteous manner. ABC COMPANY is about building relationships with our clients, making them feel like they are a part of the family, and can completely trust ABC COMPANY in every way. Our concierge professionals are all required to ensure the client's right to privacy by keeping all client information confidential, whether it is received verbally, electronically or in writing.

ABC COMPANY Potential Interview Questions

1. Tell me about yourself and your background.

2. What are your strengths? Weaknesses?

3. Why did you leave your last job?

4. How do you deal with criticism?

5. Where do you see yourself in ten years?

6. How do you deal with authority?

7. What do you think of your previous manager?

8. What is the riskiest thing you have ever done?

9. What interests you about our company?

10. How do you stay professionally current?

11. What outside activities are most significant to your personal development?

12. You mentioned you work well with a team, can you describe a situation when you had to gain cooperation from a team.

13. Tell me about a time when you had to sacrifice quality in order to meet a deadline? How did that make you feel?

14. Tell me about a time when your organizational skills made a project successful.

15. How did you handle the unexpected?

16. Now let's try to summarize our conversation. Thinking about all we've covered today, what would you say are some of your strengths, qualities both personal and professional, that make you a good prospect for us?

17. What can you offer us that other people cannot?

18. How would your colleagues or supervisor describe you?

19. What about this job attracts you? What is unattractive?

20. How long do you see yourself with us?

21. How would you describe an ideal working environment?

Role Playing Questions

How would you solve the following …

1. It's 4:00 p.m. in the afternoon and a call comes in from a frantic client who wants to get into an exclusive nightclub that evening without waiting in line. The nightclub is in another city. What would you do and how would you get them into the club? Assume that our company has never contacted this club before.

2. A call comes in from a client who needs something immediately. You have three other clients who need things at the very same time. How do you solve the problem?

3. How would you handle an extremely angry, unhappy client?

Sample Concierge Company

<u>Employee Handbook</u>

Sample Concierge Company

131 Sample Lane, Sample City, USA
Tel: 333-333-3333 Fax: 333-333-3331
Website: www.sampleconcierge.com

Dear Sample Concierge Staff:

As employees of Sample Concierge, it is important that each of you be aware of our current policies and procedures. This handbook contains easily referenced guidelines that pertain to employment policies, benefits and general information that each of you will find useful while working here.

It is our firm policy that family comes first and we will always do our best to accommodate any reasonable situation that may come up with our employees and their families.

Please remember that my door is always open for anyone who wishes to talk to me about their job, our policies, recommend changes, or ask questions of any kind.

I'm looking forward to working with you.

Sincerely,

Joseph Van Pelt
President

Table of Contents

The Corporate Policies that follow contain policies adopted by Sample Concierge, Inc. All employees of Sample Concierge, Inc. are required to adhere to the requirements of these Corporate Policies. While department policies may provide additional requirements for their employees, such policies must be consistent with and meet the requirements of the applicable Corporate Policy.

Employment Policies
>   Equal Opportunity Policy/Affirmative Action
>   Compliance
>   Statement
>   Drug-Free Workplace Statement

Conflict of Interest

Incident Policy

Sexual Harassment

Smoking

Substance Abuse

Infectious Disease Policy

Annual Performance Evaluation Form

Employee Benefits

1. *Social Security* - all employees shall participate in the social security program

2. *Workman's Compensation* - All employees shall be covered by Workman's Compensation Insurance.

3. *Unemployment Compensation* - All employees shall be covered by state and federal employment security laws.

4. *Medical/Dental/Disability Insurance* - All full-time employees shall be entitled to an individual medical/dental/disability insurance plan starting in 30 days from start date with company, or at next available start date. Employees may be required to pay a portion of their premium depending on their plan selection. New employees may be subjected to pre-existing conditions depending on insurance company policies.

5. All employees shall be eligible to participate in the 401(k) Plan. Participation is voluntary and employees are eligible to enroll in the Plan upon date of hire.

Holidays

Sample Concierge will be closed on the following holidays (except for special events):

New Year's Day, January 1
Memorial Day
Independence Day, July 4
Labor Day
Thanksgiving for 2 days

Christmas Eve Day, December 24

Christmas Day, December 25 and 2 floating holidays

Vacation Leave

Full-time employees shall be granted vacation based on their years of service with the company. The following schedule will determine the amount of leave an employee is entitled to.

After 6 months employment, employee will receive 2 days of vacation leave. This time, however, cannot be taken congruently without approval of management and cannot be carried over to the next year.

1 year	1 week
2 - 4 years	2 weeks
5 - 9 years	3 weeks
10 or more	4 weeks

Regardless of the amount of vacation employees are entitled to, employees may carry forward up to one (1) week of vacation into the following year with their supervisor's permission.

Upon retirement or termination of employment, any unused annual leave accrued shall be paid to the employee in a lump sum payment.

Personal Leave

Regular full-time employees are eligible for personal leave. Personal leave can be used when a member of the employee's immediate family requires his/her attention, when there is an emergency that only the employee can handle, bereavements not covered under funeral leave (subject to approval by Management) etc. Personal leave hours may not be carried over from one year to the next. Personal leave is not vacation leave and therefore is not intended to supplement vacation periods. Management's approval is required for personal leave hours to be used.

Personal leave shall be charged against sick leave and may not be granted in excess of accumulated sick leave. The number of hours granted would be governed by the circumstances of the case, but in no event shall they exceed 40 hours in any calendar year. Requested personal leave in excess of 40 hours in any calendar year will be charged to vacation leave until the vacation leave balance is depleted and then to leave without pay.

Military Leave

All employees who are officers or enlisted in any component of the armed forces of the United States shall, when ordered by the proper authority to active duty or service, be entitled to a leave of absence for such active service. There will be no loss of status. There will be no loss of pay for up to 20 working days per calendar year.

Sick Leave

Each employee shall receive 6 days sick leave yearly with pay after 1 year of employment. New employees will receive 3 sick days after 6 months of employment with no days taken off. Employee shall carry over a maximum of one year's worth of sick days over to the next year.

Employees must notify their supervisor each day the employee is unable to work. While the company will pay for authorized sick days, employees are expected to be honest in requesting and using sick leave. Employees suspected of abusing their sick leave benefit may be required to bring a doctor's statement for any sick leave used.

Under no circumstances should an employee claim sick leave benefits to work on another job and any abuse of this benefit will be taken into account during performance evaluations. Appropriate disciplinary action will be taken if sick leave abuse is discovered, not to exclude termination.

Funeral Leave

The purpose of funeral leave is to provide regular full-time employees with the time to attend funerals of immediate family members and to handle related affairs without disrupting income. The maximum amount of funeral leave granted for bereavement will be determined by the relationship of the employee to the deceased as listed below:

1. Each full-time employee is allowed to use up to three (3) days for deaths in the immediate family. This includes spouse, children, mother, father or sibling of the employee, grandparents, mother-in-law, father-in-law, siblings-in-law, stepparent, stepsiblings, grandparents-in-law and grandchild.
2. Each full-time employee may be granted time off from work without loss of regular pay or deductions from leave balances for attending the funeral of a relative not a member of their immediate family but not to exceed 1 work day (8 hours). This includes uncles, aunts, nieces, nephews, first generation cousins, and in-laws not defined in the above paragraph.

Maternity Leave

Sample Concierge is in compliance with the Family and Medical Leave Act of 1993. It is the policy of the company to grant an employee up to a maximum of 12 weeks of unpaid leave in any 12 month period to care for a newborn or newly adopted child, a seriously ill family member or for the employee's own serious illness. Accumulated sick leave and vacation time may be used during maternity leave.

Administrative Leave

Employees will be placed on administrative leave with pay if summoned to serve jury duty. Administrative leave for jury duty will not be charged against the employee's annual vacation, sick leave or personal leave and the employee will be entitled to any juror's pay.

Due to a subpoena as a witness (except as plaintiff or defendant) an employee will be granted administrative leave with pay.

Workweek

Sample Concierge is open from Monday through Friday. Hours will vary. Employees are allowed 1/2 to 1 hour for lunch and regular morning/afternoon breaks. Workweek will consist of 35 to 40 hours. Overtime starts after 40 hours.

Time and Attendance

A formal record of the employee's time and attendance will be maintained.

Outside Employment

A person who accepts full-time employment with Sample Concierge assumes a primary professional obligation to the company. Any other employment or enterprise in which the employee engages for income must be understood to be secondary to his work at the company. Employees may not re-arrange schedules to accommodate outside employment. Outside employment must not be a conflict of interest or have the perception of being a conflict of interest with his/her company work.

Employee will not sell or arrange any personal arrangements or business while working on company premises or while on company time.

If outside employment becomes a problem for the employee to perform his/her company work the employee will be asked to correct the problem, not to exclude the termination of the outside employment. Any employee working outside the company on a regular basis should inform his/her supervisor.

Increases in Salary

After 12 months of service and a yearly performance evaluation, employees will be eligible for advancement to a higher salary upon recommendation of the employee's immediate supervisor and upon the concurrence of the President. Annual cost-of-living increases will be granted as deemed appropriate by the Management.

A performance evaluation will be conducted every six months.

Pay Day

All salaried employees will be paid twice a month.

Termination Process

Although an employee may terminate their employment at will, the company requests an employee to give at least two weeks notice via a letter of resignation submitted to their immediate supervisor. The salary of an employee whose services are terminated before the end of the month will be prorated on the basis of workdays during the month of termination. There will be no payment for any unused accrued sick leave or vacation leave at time of termination.

Employment Policies

Equal Opportunity Policy/Affirmative Action Compliance Statement

The President and employees of Sample Concierge reaffirm the following policy:

In compliance with Title VI and Title VII of the Civil Rights Act of 1964, Executive Order 11246 as amended, Title IX of the Education Amendments of 1972, Sections 503 and 504 of the Rehabilitation Act of 1973, the Americans With Disabilities Act of 1990, the Family & Medical Leave Act of 1999, the Civil Rights Act of 1991 and other federal rules and regulations, Triangle Concierge does not discriminate on the basis of race, color, religion, gender, age, national origin, physical challenge, visual or hearing impairment, disability or status as a veteran.

Drug-Free Workplace Policy Statement

Sample Concierge, in compliance with the Drug-Free Workplace Act of 1988, hereby gives notice to all its employees that the statements listed below constitute the company's formal policy. It is in the best interests of both the Company and its employees to provide education, awareness, and assistance where appropriate relative to the dangers inherent in the unlawful manufacture, distribution, dispensation, possession or use of a controlled substance in the workplace. The special consequences of drug abuse in the workplace include the threatened safety to co-workers by those who are impaired by drugs the increased danger of defective or substandard services being provided to the public and diminished productivity.

1. The unlawful manufacture, distribution, dispensation, possession or use of a controlled substance in any company work area, or outside of company when on company time is prohibited.
2. As a condition of employment, employees must abide by the terms of this policy.
3. Any employee who is convicted of any state or federal criminal drug statue for drug-related misconduct in the workplace must report the conviction within five (5) working days to the President.
4. Violations will result in administrative sanctions, ranging in severity from formal counseling to termination of employment, immediately or within 30 days, whether or not the violation results in conviction under state and federal criminal drug statutes for misconduct in the workplace. Satisfactory participation in a company approved drug abuse assistance or rehabilitation program may be required as a condition of continued employment by the company of all employees who violate this prohibition and are not terminated from employment.

Conflict of Interest

An employee has an obligation and responsibility to report to their immediate supervisor any outside business or financial activity which is or may be in conflict with the interests of Sample Concierge or which interferes with the performance of his/her duties. Violations of this policy will be considered grounds for disciplinary action, up to and including termination.

No employee shall conduct outside business or financial activity during business hours when employee is working for Sample Concierge.

Incident Policy

Sample Concierge is committed to maintaining a workplace environment that is safe and secure for all employees of the company. Threats, threatening behavior, acts of violence and unwanted attention directed against other employees, visitors, or guests by anyone will not be tolerated.

Sexual Harassment

Sample Concierge condemns sexual harassment in any form and is committed to providing a safe environment free of it for everyone. Sexual harassment means unwelcome sexual advances, requests for sexual favors and other verbal or physical conduct of a sexual nature.

All complaints concerning sexual harassment will be thoroughly investigated, with care taken to protect the rights of the complainant as well as the rights of the alleged harasser. A finding of sexual harassment will result in appropriate disciplinary action, which may include a range of actions up to, and including dismissal. Legal actions may be taken.

Smoking

Smoking and the use of all tobacco products are prohibited in the office and in the lobby concierge set-ups.

Substance Abuse

Sample Concierge strives to ensure that all employees are provided with a supportive work environment. Therefore, the company will provide reasonable assistance for employees in dealing with personal problems such as substance abuse, including alcohol and drug abuse.

SAMPLE

PERFORMANCE EVALUATION

Employee Name:_____

Title: _____

Rating Period: From: _____   To: _____

Review Date: _____

Mid-year Review Date: _____

Procedures:

1. Supervisor identifies major skills required for job success, lists them and communicates these to employees at beginning of appraisal cycle.

2. Employee completes the self-appraisal (parts I-II) before scheduled appraisal meeting

3. Supervisor reviews employee's self-appraisal and evaluates employee's performance (parts I-IV)

4. Supervisor and employee meet for the appraisal interview to discuss their ratings, sign the evaluation form and make comments.

5. Form is reviewed and signed by the President.

Part I - Skills

The following is a list of skills which apply to this position

Skills	Not Acceptable		Partially Achieving Expectations		Achieving Expectations		Exceeding Expectations	
	Emp	Supv	Emp	Supv	Emp	Supv	Emp	Supv

Notes:

Part II – Performance Standards

Skills	Not Acceptable		Partially Achieving Expectations		Achieving Expectations		Exceeding Expectations	
	Emp	Supv	Emp	Supv	Emp	Supv	Emp	Supv
Knowledge of Job: Understanding job procedures, equipment & responsibilities								
Quantity of Work: Completing tasks thoroughly and accurately								
Dependability: Reliability to do assigned work and meet deadlines and schedules								
Coordination of Work: planning and organizing of work, tasks and use of company resources								
Judgement: Decision making and problem solving ability								
Cooperation: Willingness to accept supervisory instructions and directions and willingness to apply effort								

Skills	Not Acceptable		Partially Achieving Expectations		Achieving Expectations		Exceeding Expectations	
	Emp	Supv	Emp	Supv	Emp	Supv	Emp	Supv
Interaction with Others: Willingness & ability to get along, interact and work with others, both internally and externally								
Initiative & Enthusiasm: Self-reliance and self-starting ability								
Commitment to Job: Demonstrating a consistent, dependable work effort, and a positive work attitude								
Attendance and Punctuality: using company time conscientiously								

Mid-year Discussion

Supervisor Comments:_____

_____

_____

_____

Employee Comments: _____

_____

_____

_____

Part III: Supervisor explains any rating from Part I or II that is "not acceptable." _____

_____

_____

_____

Part IV: Overall Performance rating of employee

o   Not Acceptable
o   Partially Achieving Expectations
o   Achieving Expectation
o   Exceeding Expectations

Part V: Action Plans for Improving Performance in Present Position:

<u>Annual Review:</u>

Supervisor Comments: _____

_____

_____

_____

Employee Comments: _____

_____

_____

_____

_____   _____

Supervisor Signature   Date

_____   _____

Employee Signature   Date

Example of a Concierge Service Business Plan

Confidentiality Agreement

(To be placed on first page after cover page)

The undersigned reader acknowledges that the information provided by John Smith in this business plan is confidential and therefore reader agrees not to disclose it without the express permission of John Smith.

It is acknowledged by reader that information to be furnished in this business plan is in all respects confidential in nature, other than information which is in the public domain through other means and that any disclosure or use of same by reader, may cause serious hard or damage to Sample Concierge.

Upon request, this document is to be immediately returned to John or Karen Smith.

_____   _____
Signature   Date

_____
Name (typed or printed)

This is a business plan. It does not imply offering of securities.

Introduction

John and Karen Smith started the Sample Concierge Company in January 1999 in Sample City and plans to open its doors by August 1999. Sample Concierge was recently formed to offer both corporate and lobby concierge services to area businesses who are now offering concierge services as part of their complete human resources and employee benefits packages. As good employees become increasingly hard to find in a hot U.S. economy, businesses are looking for new and effective ways to either attract or retain their valuable staff members. As a result, the concierge business is the wave of the future, with concierge companies popping up around the country.

Area companies will be able to offer employees a host of services that include: picking up dry cleaning, running errands, managing catered business lunches, personal shopping, business referrals, and ordering dinner to name a few. Sample Concierge can buy your groceries, make your travel arrangements and arrange for a courier. Now instead of making 20 calls, the employee only has to make one. Sample Concierge employees are equipped to help our clients manage some of those nagging 'to do's' in their life, and for people who have recently relocated to the area, our company can help eliminate all the wasted time looking for appropriate providers of various basic services.

Mission Statement

Sample Concierge Company strives to offer outstanding service for busy executives in Sample City. Our mission is to place a concierge desk in the lobby of every office building in the greater Sample City area and to bring new meaning to the words "employee benefits package." We are dedicated to giving our clients some extra time by making concierge services a part of their corporate benefits package.

Companies are using concierge services to attract and retain keyemployees, as well as to increase productivity by keeping their employees at their desks during work hours. Using a concierge service benefits the employee by freeing up more time for them to enjoy doing the things they choose when the workday ends without the stress of running errands.

Changes in the U.S. workforce and an increasingly frenetic lifestyle for the family of the 90s has further fueled the trend towards use of corporate and even personal concierge services. According to a recent study of the U.S. work force released by the Families and Work Institute, the average worker:

• Spends 44 hours per week on the job
• 36 percent of workers say they often feel completely used up at the end of the workday.

And there is certainly no rest for us when we get home:

• 85% of workers have daily family responsibilities to go home to
• 78% of married workers have spouses who are also employed
• Weekends are consumed by errands and housekeeping
• 70% of all parents feel they don't spend enough time with their children.

Looking at these statistics, it's easy to see why time has become a precious commodity. The popularity of concierge services stems from the fact that people are stressed out, overworked, and need help dealing with life. Sample Concierge believes such a service will be especially useful in Sample City because there is such a large influx of transplants. Increasingly busy people want to spend what time they have with their families and nurturing themselves. They don't want to be forced to run errands. We are pleased to help bring this new national trend to companies and employees in Sample City.

Unique Features

Sample Concierge is Sample City's premier corporate concierge service. It is designed to be the ultimate stress reliever by giving you back the one thing that you never have enough of ... time.

Let's use an example of someone's typical day. It is 5:00 p.m. and after a very long day at the office (where you still need to get a computer consultant to come in) you have to fight rush find a meeting planner, organize a sales trip for your boss, and hour traffic to get home. Once in your neighborhood you have to rush to the dry cleaners, buy groceries, pick up the kids and run home to cook dinner. After dinner you have to contact the travel agent, make dinner reservations for an upcoming outing with friends, send flowers to your sick aunt and arrange to have the carpet cleaned because your 3-year-old spilled grape juice (all while being constantly interrupted by your kids).

Then your spouse reminds you that you need to plan a surprise birthday party for his mother for 50 people! Now you need a caterer, invitations and a cleaning company to come and clean your house! Oh... and don't forget you need to take a personal day tomorrow so that you can meet the washing machine repairman. Talk about stress! Not everyone has such a hectic schedule, but we all have days where we could certainly use more hours in the day (or at least a machine that could clone us so we could be in several places at once). Sample Concierge is a one-stop shop where you can send us your "to do" list and then consider it done. Instead of making hundreds of telephone calls both at the office and from home using up your valuable time, you just make one call — to us.

Your time is valuable and Sample Concierge would like to give you some more of it so that you can spend more time with your family doing things that you actually want to do instead of the things that you have to do.

Marketing Objectives

Sample Concierge's marketing strategy starts with a website, www.sampleconcierge.com. that is currently on the Internet. Another website has been designed by CitySearch and will be up by the middle of March. Two "tiles" will be placed on several feature article pages for users to click on and locate our service. A synopsis of our company is located on the Sample City Chamber of Commerce's map project, and will be available to the public in March. In addition, a mailing will be sent out to various companies in the area announcing the business. Mailings will actually be sent out on a regular basis to market the service.

Furthermore, the Sample City Chapter of Meeting Professionals International is doing an article on Mrs. Smith that should be out towards the end of March. A press release will be sent out to all the local media agencies once the first corporate client is signed on and monthly thereafter.

Concierge Services will be offered to area employees as part of a corporate benefits package or as a payroll deduction. Sample Concierge will set-up appointments with human resources departments and corporate managers and will present our unique and professional services to them.

Additional and continuous marketing such as radio spots, magazine and newspaper advertisements will be considered as revenue increases.

Expected Accomplishments

Sample Concierge expects increased continuous revenue with profitability by the second year. The table (goals) shown below represents a five-year projection of the company's rate of growth.

Table 1

The numbers listed below are an example only and are not an actual representation

Description	Year 1	Year 2	Year 3	Year 4	Year 5
Gross Sales	$45,000	135,000	202,000	252,600	290,000
Growth Rate	—	300%	50%	25%	15%

Required Capital

In order for Sample Concierge to commence its operations, $115,000 will be needed. An investment of $20,000 will be required from each owner (numbers here are just samples). The owners of Sample Concierge will need to contribute $20,000 of their own funds and will require financing from a lender for an additional $75,000. The business requires a 3-year loan that will be repaid in monthly installments.

THE BUSINESS

Problem Statement

People have too much to do and not enough time in which to do it. That is today's basic problem. Sample Concierge aims to solve this problem by doing some of the everyday tasks for the client.

In today's market, companies and individuals do not have the time to do all the items they have on their "to do" list and still be able to spend some quality time with their families. Furthermore, if they need to plan a meeting or event they do not always have the time or the expertise to put it together on top of everything else they need to do. Shopping around for travel agents, caterers, florists, photographers, rental companies and musicians for an event takes a significant amount of time. On top of everything else, it is hard to find the time to pick up/deliver dry cleaning, find courier services, solve computer problems, locate a particular type of restaurant and find a good service repairman.

Having an intermediary who has done the research for them and has established a relationship with these businesses can be invaluable. Customers actually have two choices: they can do everything themselves, or they can hire someone to help them.

The question then becomes how much you value your time. Sample Concierge can meet all your needs under the same roof. We are a one-stop shop so that our clients can make ONE phone call instead of hundreds thus saving them both time and money.

Description of the Business

Sample Concierge will do everything on a client's "to do" list for a reasonable yearly membership fee. The partners intend to target area companies as its source of business. These companies will in turn offer concierge services to their employees as part of their corporate benefits packages. Sample Concierge has reliable and honest vendors available and has negotiated discounts with them for their clients.

Furthermore, each vendor promises to give Sample Concierge a 10% referral fee. This allows us to charge reasonable yearly membership rates. Our corporate office is open from 9:00 a.m to 5:00 p.m. Monday through Friday.

We will offer our clients the following services ... instead of running around during your lunch hour, fighting crowds on Saturday or racing around after 5 ... let us do your errands for you. We can pick up your dry cleaning, buy your groceries... whatever your needs are.

Sample Concierge can order all of your tickets for concerts, sporting events, holiday events, Broadway shows, or the ballet. We can arrange for your golf tee times, reserve a tennis court for you, arrange for you to go horseback riding or make a reservation for you to take a scuba diving lesson.

We can give you some dinner recommendations/reservations, arrange for a limousine, town car, bus, helicopter or charter plane. We can send flowers to that special someone for you, or can order arrangements for that special event. Let us help you find a DJ, band, magician, clown, comedian, impersonator or book a celebrity for your special event. Sample Concierge can also help you with your Airline Reservations, Hotel/Motel Reservations, Ground Transportation, Vacation Rentals, Resort Recommendations/Reservations, and

Relocation Services. Plus we can assist your employees with their relocation! We can arrange for Short Term Condo/Apartment Rentals, Airlines and Rental Car Reservations, Movers and Storage.

Clients are more than welcome to access our Business Referral List and obtain a referral for virtually anything ... from Childcare, Maids and Cleaning Professionals to Moving and Storage Companies.

History of the Business

Sample Concierge was formed in January 1999 in Sample City by two equal partners, John and Karen Smith, who hold equal shares in the company. After reading an article in Entrepreneur Magazine and searching the Internet it was discovered that Sample City had no corporate concierge company. They realized that John's sales and marketing experience combined with Karen's meeting and event-planning talent would make them the perfect team. They came up with a concierge service that targets both individual residents and area companies.

Founder(s) of the Business

The combined talents of the two partners John and Karen create the uniqueness of this service. John has been in the sales and marketing and customer service fields for over 20 years and Karen has worked as a meeting planner for over 15 years, and has planned all types of meetings, events and exhibits across the country.

Management & Operations

John currently runs the business. He is also responsible for the sales and marketing of the company and is responsible for all the financial matters. Karen runs the operations.

William Douglas is the company's accountant and bookkeeper. There are two full-time errand drivers, three part-time drivers, a night operations manager and an in-office administrative assistant.

Partners are allowed two weeks vacation, just not at the same time. Partners can expect a salary once the company begins to show a profit. Employees will be hired as needed. Prior to the hiring of the first employee, partners will establish an employee handbook and benefit plan.

Regulations & Licensing

No licensing is required. Liability insurance is being looked into. Meeting Insurance is obtained on a meeting by meeting basis. Both Service Vendors and Members sign a basic liability contract when they sign on.

Objectives

It is Sample Concierge's objective to be able to meet its expenses by the end of August 1999. It is expected to show a profit by January 2000. In order to do this we will market the business through our two websites as well as direct-mail campaigns. Furthermore, we will obtain corporate clients by cold-calling various human resources departments, networking events and mailings.

SERVICE

Service Description

Sample Concierge is a one-stop shop designed to provide customers with an array of services.

These include errand service, personal shopping, travel assistance, relocation services, meeting and event planning and our business referral service.

Related Products

It is not our intention to sell specific products, however, we will promote companies that offer various services and products that we feel our clients will value.

MARKETING

Objectives & Strategies

Sample Concierge has set its marketing objectives by targeting the human resources departments of area companies. An aggressive direct mail campaign as well as direct telephone calls to area companies will be used. Advertisements will be placed in local newspapers and magazines. A press release will be mailed out to all area media agencies. Finally, partners will attend as many Sample City Chamber of Commerce networking functions as possible to network with area company representatives.

Unique Selling Advantage

Sample Concierge is available whenever the client needs us.... our errand service is here 24 hours a day, 7 days a week via fax, telephone and e-mail.

Channels of Distribution

Sample Concierge intends to utilize its wide network of independent contractors to provide its services. The owners have obtained a written agreement from each service vendor who have agreed to provide the various services and give Sample Concierge a 10% commission on each sale.

Pricing

Sample Concierge offers a yearly membership fee that ranges from $200 to $1,500 per year depending upon the type of package, number of employees and services required. Clients are also charged an hourly rate for our errand and personal shopping service. Meeting and event planning is quoted on a per event basis and depends on the type of event, how many people, location, and how long it will take to put the function together for the client. Service vendors also give Sample Concierge a 10% commission.

Table 2

COMPANY	Commissions	% Variation from Market
Sample Errand Co.	10% - 15%	10% - 15%
Sample Concierge Co.	7% to 10%	7% to 10%

ADVERTISING

Advertising will concentrate on print advertising in the Yellow Pages, various magazines, newspapers and direct mail. The advertising budget will be 4% of the gross sales in the first and second year. The percentage increases to 6% thereafter.

Table 3
ADVERTISING

Type of Media	January	February	March	April
Yellow Pages	$412	$412	$412	$412
Business Leader Magazine	0	1,200	1,200	1,200
The Sample City Times	800	800	800	800
Direct Mail	500	500	500	500
TOTAL SPENDING	$1,712	$2,912	$2,912	$2,912

Publicity & Public Relations

Sample Concierge will send out a press release to all the local media agencies. At present, no budget has been allocated for public relations since it will be done by the owners through networking.

FINANCES

Start-Up Costs

An initial investment will be required in order for Sample Concierge to commence business. A budget of the company's required resources has been compiled in the following table. *The following numbers are not accurate representations of the current market and are for demonstration purposes only.*

Table 4
START-UP COSTS

COST	AMOUNT
Salaries for two individuals	$50,000
Inventory	$2,500
Furniture and Equipment	$5,000
Rent for 3 months	$1,500
Utilities	$5,000
Legal and Professional Fees	$10,000
Advertising and Promotions	$10,000
Miscellaneous	$1,000
TOTAL START-UP COSTS	$85,000

Sources & Uses of Capital

In order for Sample Concierge to successfully start operations, a total investment of $115,000 will be needed. The owners will each contribute $20,000 of their own money and will require an additional $75,000 from a lender. The business will require a 3-year loan that will be repaid in monthly installments.

Table 5
SOURCES AND USES OF CAPITAL

SOURCES

Business Loan	$75,000
Owner Investment	$40,000
TOTAL SOURCES	$115,000

USES

Start-up Costs	$85,000
Working capital	$10,000
Reserve for contingencies	$20,000
TOTAL USES	$115,000